Keepsake

SIGNATURE QUILTS

American Quilter's Society

P. O. Box 3290 • Paducah, KY 42002-3290
www.AQSquilt.com

Located in Paducah, Kentucky, the American Quilter's Society (AQS) is dedicated to promoting the accomplishments of today's quilters. Through its publications and events, AQS strives to honor today's quiltmakers and their work and to inspire future creativity and innovation in quiltmaking.

EDITOR: JANE TOWNSWICK
TECHNICAL EDITOR: SHELLEY HAWKINS
GRAPHIC DESIGN: AMY CHASE
COVER DESIGN: MICHAEL BUCKINGHAM
PHOTOGRAPHY: CHARLES R. LYNCH

Library of Congress Cataloging-in-Publication Data
Saulmon, Sally
    Keepsake signature quilts / by Sally Saulmon.
      p. cm.
     ISBN 1-57432-816-6
    1. Patchwork--Patterns. 1. Quilting--Patterns. 1. Signatures
(Writing) I. Title.

    TT835.S267 2003
     746.46'041--dc21

                               2003004235
                               CIP

Additional copies of this book may be ordered from the American Quilter's Society, PO Box 3290, Paducah, KY 42002-3290; 800-626-5420 (orders only please); or online at www.AQSquilt.com. For all other inquiries, call 270-898-7903.

Dedication

This book is dedicated to the memory of my grandmothers:
Grandma Haines, Mother Billingslea, Great-grandmother
DeLong, and Great-grandmother Maddex. They taught me that
the best part of the day was after the gardening and housework
were done. Then you could sit down and do your "fancywork."

Sally Saulmon with her grandmothers

Detail of FOUR-PATCH quilt

FOUR-PATCH, 37" x 30", made by the
author in 1950. This doll quilt was
made of scraps from the dresses and
aprons of Sally's grandmothers.

Acknowledgments

Thanks, with love, to my husband, Bob, who has given

me the ultimate luxury of staying home all of these

years to build our nest, to raise our children, and to

quilt. To Mike and Jenni, thanks for teaching me every

day what is important in life. Caitlin, I'm so glad you

agreed to share your playroom with my sewing

machine. I would also like to acknowledge Terri Lynn

Ballard, Nancy Grove, and Bobbie A. Aug for their

encouragement. The editorial assistance of Barbara

Smith and Jane Townswick has been invaluable. And

without all of those friends and acquaintances that

have contributed signatures to the quilts, this book

could not have been conceived.

Contents

Foreword

Thankfully, quiltmakers have numerous opportunities to design and create signature quilts to document family histories, friendships, patriotism, and special events. These textiles nurture personal relationships and foster community involvement.

Through time, quilt styles evolved from whole-cloth to medallion, then four-block to multiple-block construction. The increased complexity of a block quilt allowed many hands to participate in the assembly of a quilt top. At the same time, a profusion of signatures, verses, and inscriptions were created in the 1800s, and indelible ink became more reliable. The simultaneous development of these factors paved the way for signature quilts. Autograph albums began showing up in parlors in 1830 after being featured in *Godey's Lady's Book* magazine. Following closely on its heels, the album block quilt debuted in the early 1840s on the East Coast.

Signature quilts can be made for males as well as females. However, signature quilts historically were made by women for women. Men could and did participate by signing blocks. Appreciation and encouragement for this style of documentation and commemoration continues today and makes people aware of the value of quilts as family history and material culture.

It is an honor to be asked to sign a piece of muslin or a block that will eventually become a part of someone's cherished quilt. To know that something of us will live on long after we have left this earth is wonderfully comforting. Sally Saulmon gives us many opportunities to enjoy this experience when we participate in making keepsake signature quilts.

Signature quilts celebrate the efforts of many quiltmakers. These quilts often present an intriguing picture of the people who participated in making them and chronicle the fabrics and politics of the times. As in the past, these quilts are treasured and seldom used as bed covers. They are truly keepsakes.

Introduction

Quilts that feature inscriptions have long been a popular tradition in quiltmaking. These special keepsakes preserve forever in cloth remembrances of friends and family and warm feelings of affection and friendship. A wonderful legacy of signature quilts has come to us from the beautiful 1830s album and friendship quilts, the Victorian crazy quilts, and the many lovely presentation and fundraiser quilts of the twentieth century.

A signature quilt is any quilt that contains blocks with signatures or inscriptions. It may display names of friends or family, autographs of famous people, phrases of friendship and feelings, or even drawings of meaningful objects. Signature quilts have long been made to commemorate and celebrate many occasions, such as births, graduations, marriages, or anniversaries. Presentation quilts with signatures and inscribed messages have often been given to someone by a group of people wishing to express thanks for service and dedication.

In the nineteenth and early twentieth centuries, fundraising signature quilts, such as the LADIES' AID SOCIETY FUNDRAISING QUILT on page 8, were popular. By obtaining donations from people for the privilege of having their names appear on this type of quilt, groups could raise funds for various causes. When the completed quilts were sold at auction, still more money could be raised. Such quilts were often the only arena where women were allowed to express their personal or patriotic views.

In the past, blocks for signature quilts were often assembled by one person, with guests signing a patch of fabric to be included in each block. Sometimes signed blocks were collected from individual quiltmakers and presented to an honored recipient, who assembled the quilt at a later time. Often a completed quilt top was quilted at a group quilting party. One of the most traditional aspects of quiltmaking was the sense of camaraderie and lasting friendship among women who participated in quilting bees. Thus, signature quilts became treasured souvenirs of shared time and memories.

Today, as in the past, signature quilts are still being made by quiltmakers everywhere. In addition to being expressions of our sentiments, these quilts function as lasting documents of our thoughts and feelings, providing insights that speak to us personally. As Linda Otto Lipsett says in her book, *Remember Me*, "...in piecing blocks, gathering signatures, and signing cloth we are connecting with women's spirit of the past. Despite time and change, we still find great satisfaction in signing our names in friendship onto cloth."

On the following pages, you will find guidelines for planning a keepsake signature quilt, hints and tips on choosing fabrics and color palettes, methods for inking fabric, and ideas for organizing the process of making and finishing the quilt. The twenty-four block patterns are designed to be signature blocks. I hope you enjoy using them to create unique signature quilts of your own, and enjoy continuing the legacy of these special quilts.

Sally Saulmon

BREWSTER ALBUM PATCH, *90" x 91", 1847. This quilt was assembled in Manchester, New Hampshire, by Mrs. J. K. Brewster. It contains many signatures, and one can only guess the story this quilt could tell. From the collection of the Canon City, Colorado, Municipal Museum. Donated* by W. R. Fanning, great-grandson of Mr. Brewster, founder of the small community of Brewster, near Canon City. Photo by Beel Photography, Canon City, Colorado.

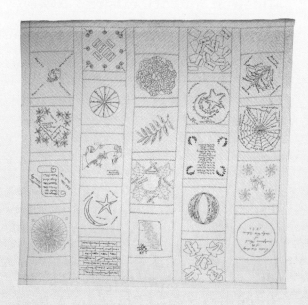

LADIES' AID SOCIETY FUNDRAISING QUILT, *80" x 82", 1906. As a fundraising effort, the ladies of the Presbyterian Church of Rocky Ford, Colorado, obtained donations from members of the church for the privilege of having their names embroidered on the quilt. Some blocks contain names of those in a specific Sunday school class, while other blocks were purchased by families. This quilt was evidently auctioned to raise more money, as it was discovered recently in an antique shop in northern Colorado and returned to the Rocky Ford Presbyterian Church. At one time, all of the author's grandmothers were members of this Ladies' Aid Society. Photo by Lex Nichols Photography, Rocky Ford, Colorado.*

Signature Quilt Planning

With today's busy lifestyles, carrying on the tradition of signature quilts requires significant planning. Coordinating a group project requires time and diplomacy, but it can also be an opportunity to share a wonderful experience with old and new friends or family members. To aid in making the following decisions, consider the time available to the people in your group, as well as the range of the participants' abilities.

Determining the Purpose

Deciding the purpose of the proposed quilt is the first step in planning a signature quilt. Start by asking yourself some of the following questions:

- Will the quilt be a thank-you gift to be given for service in office or on a committee?

- Will the quilt be a remembrance quilt for someone moving to another location?

- Will the quilt be made to celebrate a specific occasion, such as a birth, anniversary, wedding, or other type of special get-together?

Block and Setting Options

Because the majority of signature quilts are made as group projects, the block format is the easiest to organize and accomplish. The most popular designs are usually blocks that are set straight or on-point, with plain or pieced sashing. Alternating blocks and strippy sets are traditional favorites as well. Innovative settings, such as offset blocks in zigzag sets or floating sets, can also be beautiful.

Consider the participants' abilities. If your group is small, with a wide range of skill levels, consider a design that accommodates everyone's abilities and interests, such as an album quilt in which every block is different. Both patchwork and appliqué blocks may be featured. If your group is large, a simple patchwork quilt with a repeat-block format is often the most successful. However, you may choose an album block format or an innovative setting. The most trouble-free project for a large group is one that can be kept simple.

The block patterns on pages 19–108 are suitable for quiltmakers with beginning to intermediate skill levels. As you look through them to decide which ones might work best for your group, think about the information or messages the signature blocks will feature. Will names be included? Dates? Personalized inscriptions? Drawings? Select a block or blocks with signature areas large enough to accommodate the information you wish to convey.

Selecting Fabrics

Just as for any other type of quilt, planning the color scheme for a signature quilt takes time and thought. Take the following ideas into consideration and choose the ones that are most suitable for your project.

If the signature quilt is not intended as a surprise, it is helpful to consult the recipient in advance regarding color and fabric preferences. Consider assigning different colors or values to various pattern pieces within your block. That way, each participant can choose his or her own fabrics for each block. This method produces a quilt that has a wide variety of different fabrics, while maintaining a unified look in the placement of light and dark fabrics in the blocks.

Another option for choosing fabrics is for an individual or a committee to select the fabrics for the quilt ahead of time, and distribute them to each of the participants. This will create a planned color scheme in which each block is identical.

Another way to unify a signature quilt is to feature a theme fabric in every block. This can be included with each participant's own fabrics. A theme fabric can be any fabric that speaks to the recipient's interests. For example, a cowboy fabric may be included in a quilt for someone who owns a ranch. For a gardener, you might include a floral fabric featuring his or her favorite flowers.

Signatures and inscriptions read best on light, solid fabric; however, this does not preclude the use of medium solids or tone-on-tone prints. If the same fabric is used for the signature areas in every block, the result will be a unified look throughout the finished quilt.

Signing the Blocks

Consider the time involved and the needs and abilities of your group in deciding which signature method will work best for your quilt. Both of the following options produce beautiful signature quilts:

- Distribute individual patches to many people for inking. These people may include both quilters and non-quilters.

- A single person can sign and/or inscribe the patches for all of the blocks in the quilt. Because the same hand does all of the writing, this process produces a unified look in the finished quilt.

Constructing the Blocks

In determining how to construct individual signature blocks, consider both of the following options:

- A group of individuals or members of a committee can work together to assemble the blocks for a signature quilt, whether the blocks are identical or each are different patterns.

- One person may make all of the signature blocks for the quilt, whether they are the same or different patterns. This can be a thought-provoking process. For example, a quilt with genealogical information is sure to become a family keepsake, as well as an opportunity for the quiltmaker to learn about family history. Making a signature quilt can also be helpful in understanding many other life passages.

Assembling the Quilt Top

Decide which of the following options will work best for the signature quilt you want to make:

- One person may assemble all of the blocks into the finished quilt top.

- A committee or designated group of quilters may work together to assemble the blocks into the quilt top.

Quilting and Finishing

Either of the following options can be taken for quilting and finishing the signature quilt:

- A single quilter may do all of the quilting and finishing, either by hand or machine. This person may wish to donate the time involved, or a group may hire someone at a mutually determined hourly fee.

- A group or committee may work together to quilt and finish the quilt, especially if it will be hand quilted. It is helpful if all of the people who participate in hand quilting share similar skill levels and consistency in stitch length.

Signature Methods

In the past, methods for writing on signature blocks were limited to ink, stamps, stencils, and hand embroidery. Today's technology offers many new options, such as the use of computers, photocopiers, and embroidery machines. In addition, we have available a larger variety of stencils and stamps than ever before. Experiment with the following options for inking fabrics for signature blocks to decide which ones work best for your situation.

Pens

A wide variety of pens suitable for writing on fabric are available in quilt shops. Look for a pen that is permanent, fade resistant, and waterproof. You can choose from a range of many beautiful colors, including sepia tones suitable for an antique look. Pens that contain archival ink, which is acid-free, are best. Point sizes range from extra-fine, which is good for writing script, to broad tips or brush tips, which are great for shading or coloring in drawings. The leaf wreath in the block, Another Time, Another Place, was inked with a brush pen.

When considering point sizes, keep in mind that the smaller the number, the finer the point will be. Experiment with several different point sizes to find the pen or pens that work best for your needs. Before you test any pen, stabilize the fabric by ironing it onto a piece of freezer paper or placing it on top of a sandpaper board.

Always test any fabric pen you are considering on your chosen fabric, and follow the manufacturer's care and handling directions. If you

tend to write with a particularly heavy hand, you may find that some fabric pens tend to bleed more than others. Most manufacturers recommend that after the inking process is finished, you heat-set the fabric with an iron on the cotton setting.

Another Time, Another Place block, made by the author

Stencils

In the nineteenth century, tinsmiths cut stencils with a name and decoration to be used on fabric or paper. While this particular art form has been lost, a large variety of commercial plastic and metal stencils are available today for decorating friendship quilt blocks. Stencil paint is suitable for fabric application, but may make the fabric stiff. A better method is to use multipurpose stamp-pad ink that is suitable for fabric. It is acid-free, non-toxic, and may be easily applied with a stencil brush. It will work best on 100% cotton fabric, and it must be heat-set to cure the ink. It is permanent and will not fade with washing. The ABC Delight block is an example of this type of application.

sonalized rubber stamps made of your own signature or a handwritten inscription. Multipurpose stamp-pad ink labeled as suitable for fabric comes in a variety of colors. Be sure to test this product on your fabric, and follow the manufacturer's directions. The signature on the Happy the Home block was done with a rubber stamp.

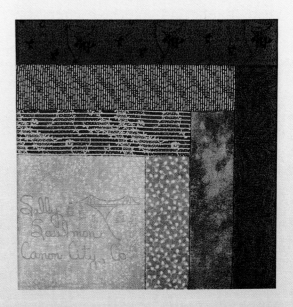

Happy the Home block, made by the author

Computers

Personal computers with scanners and ink-jet printers have opened a world of possibilities for inking fabrics. Even those of us who have limited computer knowledge can produce great results. You can scan and print your own signature, or do the same with clip-art and other copyright-free designs. Any text that can be originated in a word processing program can be used to create a

ABC Delight block, made by the author

Stamps

Rubber stamps are great to use for inscriptions on friendship blocks. Without too much searching, you can find an appropriate rubber stamp for almost any occasion. At a reasonable cost, you can have per-

signature patch. First experiment with different fonts and various colors on your computer to decide how you want your name or inscription to appear.

You can purchase 8½-by-11-inch printer-fabric sheets (see Resources, page 109), which are bonded to a removable paper backing. This fabric is washable and colorfast when you follow the manufacturer's directions. Any image printed on this type of fabric sheet will be sharp and stable, with no bleeding. However, the fabric is stiffer than off-the-bolt, 100% cotton fabric.

If you want to print on 100% cotton fabric, pretreat it by saturating it in a formaldehyde-based solution (see Resources), which will bond the dye molecules to the fibers permanently. Be sure to follow manufacturer's directions, and keep in mind that whenever you deal with chemicals, eye protection and rubber gloves are essential. After allowing it to dry, iron the fabric to the smooth side of a piece of freezer paper. Then cut the bonded fabric to 8½ x 11 inches, so that it will go through a printer. After you print your message, allow the ink to dry for approximately thirty minutes. Machine wash and rinse it in a product containing anionic surfactants (see Resources), following the manufacturer's directions. This will keep the excess dye from redepositing on the fabric. These products produce a good, permanent print, as shown in the Mountain Memories block inscription.

Mountain Memories block, made by the author

Photocopiers

Commercial photocopiers are widely available for public use, and with care and preparation, you can photocopy almost anything on fabric. Use either commercial printer fabric sheets or 100% cotton fabric prepared with a formaldehyde-based product. Feed the prepared sheets into the photocopier carefully to avoid blurring the image. The resulting print will not be as dark as the original image, but it will be both stable and permanent.

Photocopy of the author's signature on fabric

Hand Embroidery

Hand embroidery has been popular intermittently through the years for signature quilts. Victorian crazy quilts, early twentieth-century fundraising quilts, and friendship quilts of the 1930s and 1940s often contained hand embroidery. The most common stitches for signatures or inscriptions were a simple outline stitch, the chain stitch, or cross-stitching. You can use a very fine-point permanent pen or a sharp pencil to write a guideline signature on a fabric patch and then embroider it with two strands of floss or fine pearl cotton. Signatures or inscriptions may be embellished with any desired motif, such as the daisy in the Tulip Time block. Antique Victorian crazy quilts are a great source of inspiration for fanciful embroidery on quilts.

Machine Embroidery

Today's wonderful sewing machines have amazing capabilities, including the ability to embroider. Among the features are hand-guided, embroidered signatures, or programmed signatures using the machine's built-in alphabets. Any sewing machine with digitizing software capability can produce an exact replica of your signature in embroidery. A variety of threads and programmed motifs will help you create an unlimited variety of blocks suitable for a signature quilt.

Tulip Time block with embroidery, made by the author

The author's signature was digitized, then embroidered by machine.

The Quiltmaking Process

When many people work together to make a signature quilt, organization is the key to success. Use the following guidelines and ideas to organize the participants in your group and make the quiltmaking process fun for everyone involved.

Creating an Instruction Sheet

It is helpful to distribute written instructions to ensure block consistency within the group. The clearer your instructions, the better the finished results will be. Use the following ideas to create an instruction sheet that is applicable to the needs of your group, and refer to page 17 for a sample instruction sheet.

1. Start with a short paragraph that explains the reasons for making the quilt. In the event that sets of blocks or a finished quilt will be given as a prize in a drawing, state the rules involved. For example, will the winner need to be present at the drawing in order to win? Can one person be allowed to win more than one set of blocks? When and where will the drawing be held? If the blocks or quilt are to be presented as a gift, is the intention to surprise the recipient? If the blocks or quilt are made in celebration of a group event, such as a family reunion, what will happen to the finished quilt?

2. Give exact block dimensions, including seam allowances.

3. Describe the color palette and fabric choices. State the type of fabric and tell if it should be washed prior to making the blocks.

4. Provide specific instructions about signing the blocks. Include the brand names of specific pens to be used, as well as appropriate guidelines for inking fabric successfully. If you wish to leave the signature method up to each individual, state this clearly.

5. List the date when completed blocks are due, as well as the location to which they must be taken or sent. If one person will be collecting all of the blocks, list the contact information.

6. Include a diagram of the block to be made, with letters and fabric choices labeled on each patch. Include any full-sized patterns necessary, as well as specific rotary cutting instructions.

Sample Instruction Sheet

PRESIDENT'S QUILT FOR (RECIPIENT'S NAME)

The members of (**guild name**) are invited to make a block for a signature quilt to thank (**recipient's name**) for her year of service as our president. Hopefully, this will be a surprise, so we appreciate keeping this in confidence. The block, Daylight into Darkness, was chosen because (**recipient's**) friendship and vitality certainly introduce daylight into darkness. The finished block size is 6 x 6 inches. The block is to be made from a variety of dark blue print fabrics of your own choosing, plus a light blue print fabric, which will be furnished in this packet. Please use prewashed 100-percent cotton fabric. The light blue fabric, pattern pieces A, are to be signed with your name and town. Use a blue, fine-line permanent pen recommended for writing on fabric. If you do not have such a pen available, you will have an opportunity to sign your block when you turn it in. Hint: before sewing your block, stabilize the signature rectangle by ironing it to freezer paper. Sign the rectangle, remove the paper, and complete construction of the block. Blocks are due to (**contact name and phone**) by (**due date**). If you have any questions or problems, please contact her.

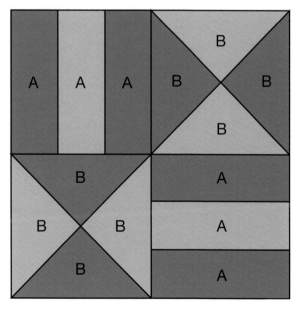

Daylight into Darkness

Fabric	Pieces
Light blue	Two 3½" x 1½" signature A rectangles One 4¼" x 4¼" square, cut in quarters diagonally, for four B triangles
Assorted dark blue	Four 3½" x 1½" A rectangles One 4¼" x 4¼" square, cut in quarters diagonally, for four B triangles

The Quiltmaking Process

Putting It All Together

Because sewing machines and methods vary, it is difficult for a large number of quiltmakers to make blocks with identical measurements. As finished blocks are received, they should be measured to determine whether any minor adjustments need to be made. For blocks that are a little too large, you can trim the edges slightly without distorting the pattern. In other cases, making a small adjustment to one or more seams may be all that is necessary. For blocks that are too small, a narrow strip of the same or similar fabric may be added to the four sides of the block to extend it. Be creative and diplomatic, keeping in mind that individual characteristics can add greatly to the charm of a group-made quilt.

A group sewing day can be a fun and rewarding experience for all. Allow the participants to choose the tasks with which they feel most comfortable. Some people may enjoy cutting sashing strips, alternate blocks, or borders, while others may wish to sew rows of blocks together. Still others may prefer to press seam allowances. You may find that some people would like to furnish lunch or snacks for everyone. Don't forget to ask someone to document the day in photos. Along with the finished quilt, a scrapbook featuring these photos, information about the quiltmaking process, and thoughts from the quiltmakers is a wonderful gift for the recipient.

Keepsake Signature Blocks

The quantities presented in each of the cutting charts represent one block, or blocks 1 and 2 in some cases. Extra triangles may result when cutting half- and quarter-square triangles.

To make enough blocks for a signature quilt, determine how many of each patch will be needed for the number of blocks in your quilt and base your yardage calculations on that information.

ABC Delight

Finished Block Size: 4" x 4"

ABC Delight is a block design that is suitable for family reunions. The signature patches may be signed by everyone attending, and easily assembled into a quilt to be raffled at the next family get-together.

⚛ Cutting ⚛

Fabric	Pieces
Gray print	One 3½" x 3½" A signature square
Black print	One 1½" x 3½" B rectangle One 1⅞" x 1⅞" square, cut in half diagonally, for two C triangles
Red print	One 1½" x 3½" B rectangle One 1⅞" x 1⅞" square, cut in half diagonally, for two C triangles

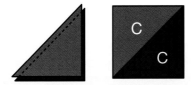

Figure 1. Sew a black and red C triangle together.

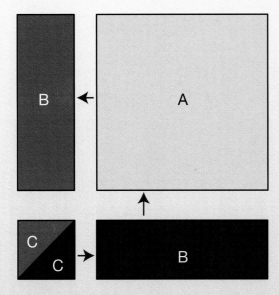

Figure 2. Block assembly

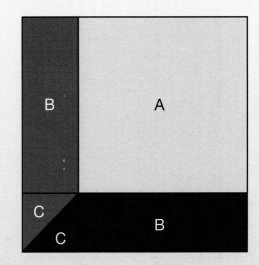

ABC Delight

🙠 *Assembly* 🙢

1. Sign the gray A square as desired, referring to Signature Methods on pages 12–15. Take care to stay inside the ¼" seam allowances.

2. Sew a black and red C triangle right sides together along the long edges to form a square (Fig. 1). Press the seam allowances toward the black triangle.

3. Assemble the patches in the order shown (Fig. 2). Press the seams in the direction of the arrows. Trim the seam allowance of the dark fabric to ⅛" if it shows through the light fabric.

ABC Delight

ABC DELIGHT, *27" x 27", made by the author. The blocks in this quilt contain words starting with the letters A through Z. The quilt is sashed and bordered with a striped fabric.*

Detail of signature area in ABC DELIGHT

Another Time, Another Place

Finished Block Size: 8" x 8"

The number of rectangles in this Courthouse Square variation can be adjusted to accommodate different sizes of signature patches.

❦ Cutting ❦

Fabric	Pieces
Beige	One 4½" x 4½" signature A square
Assorted brown and rust plaids	Two 1½" x 4½" rectangles (pieces 1 and 2) Four 1½" x 6½" rectangles (pieces 3, 4, 5, and 6) Two 1½" x 8½" rectangles (pieces 7 and 8)

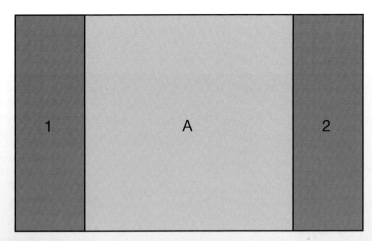

Figure 3. Sew pieces 1 and 2 to the A square.

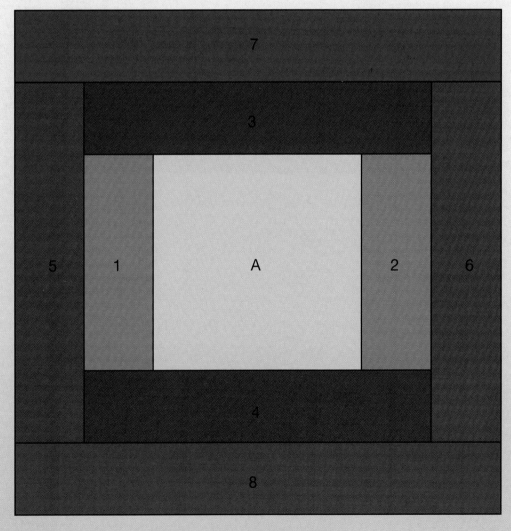

Another Time, Another Place

❧ Assembly ❧

1. Sign the A square as desired, referring to Signature Methods on pages 12–15. Take care to stay inside the ¼" seam allowances.

2. Sew plaid piece 1 to the side of the A square. Press the seam allowance toward piece 1. Sew plaid piece 2 to the opposite side of the A square. Press the seam allowance toward piece 2 (Fig. 3, page 24).

3. Continue to add pieces 3 through 8 in numerical order, completing the block. Press all seam allowances away from the A square.

Detail of signature area in ANOTHER TIME, ANOTHER PLACE, *page 26*

Another Time, Another Place

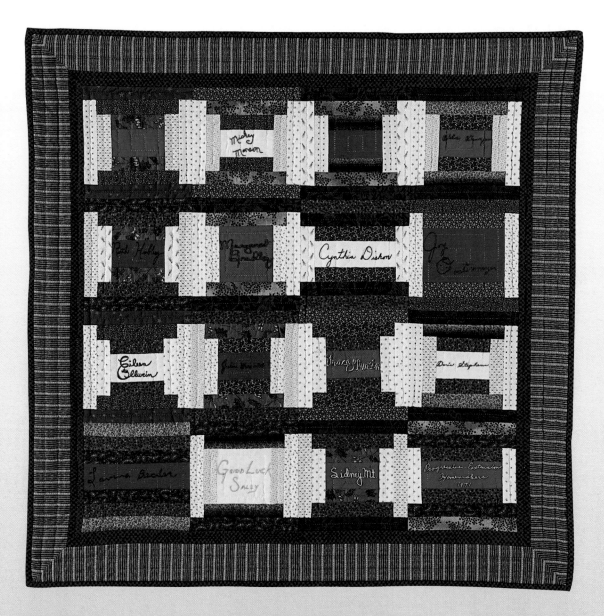

ANOTHER TIME, ANOTHER PLACE, *40" x 40", made by the author. This quilt was completed thirty years after receiving the embroidered signatures as a going-away remembrance. The signatures were different sizes and on different sizes of fabric. The block, Another Time, Another Place, was selected because the interior of the block around the signature can be adjusted to different sizes, depending on the number of rectangles added.*

Finished Block Size: 8" x 8"

You can duplicate the antique BREWSTER ALBUM PATCH quilt on page 8 by using reproduction fabrics and setting the blocks on-point, with 2¼" finished sashing. The original quilt contains sixty blocks.

❧❧ Cutting ❧❧

Fabric	Pieces
Beige	One 3⅜" x 3⅜" signature A square
Red print	Four of Template B
Teal print	One 5¼" x 5¼" C square, cut in quarters diagonally, for four C triangles

Template is on page 29.

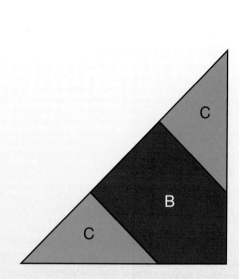

Figure 4. Unit 1 assembly, make two.

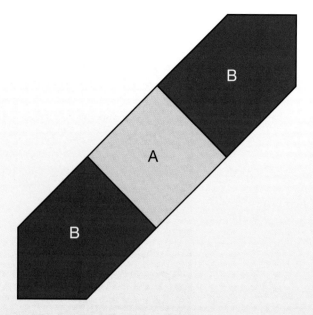

Figure 5. Unit 2 assembly, make one.

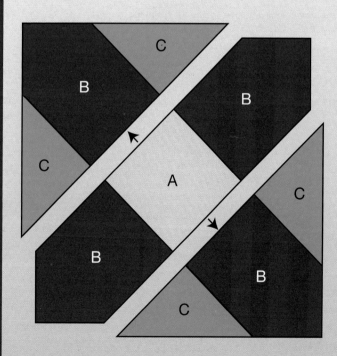

Figure 6. Block assembly

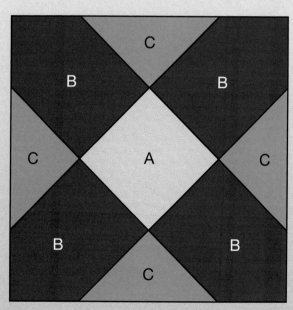

Brewster Album Patch

❧ Assembly ❧

1. Sign the A square as desired, referring to Signature Methods on pages 12–15. Take care to stay inside the ¼" seam allowances.

2. Sew a teal C triangle to each side of a red B piece as shown (Fig. 4, page 28). Press the seam allowances toward the C triangles, completing Unit 1. Make two of Unit 1.

3. Sew a red B piece to each side of the A square as shown (Fig. 5). Press the seam allowances toward the A square, completing Unit 2.

4. Sew Unit 1 to each side of Unit 2 as shown, completing the block (Fig. 6). Press the seam allowances in the direction of Unit 1.

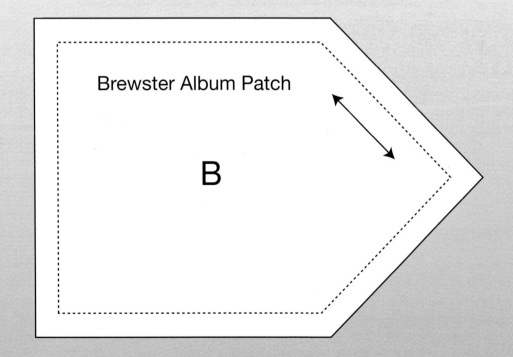

Brewster Album Patch

B

Calling Card

Finished Block Size: 6" x 6"

A versatile block, Calling Card can look very different, depending on how you use fabrics. This design is effective in an innovative setting, such as offset blocks.

ᏳᏳ Cutting ᏳᏳ

Fabric	Pieces
Pale yellow print	One 4½" x 2½" A signature rectangle Two 1½" x 2½" B rectangles
Gold-pink stripe	Four 1½" x 2½" B rectangles
Gold print	Two 2⅞" x 2⅞" C squares
Pink print	Two 2⅞" x 2⅞" C squares

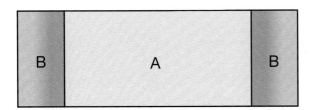

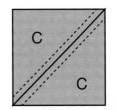

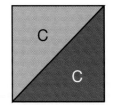

Figure 7. Sew a B rectangle to each side of the A rectangle.

Figure 8. Make four half-square triangle units.

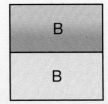

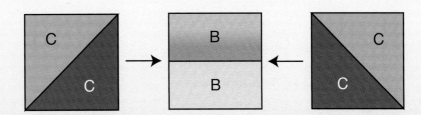

Figure 9. Sew the stripe B rectangles to the pale yellow B rectangles. Make two.

Figure 10. Sew the half-square triangles units and B/B units together. Make two.

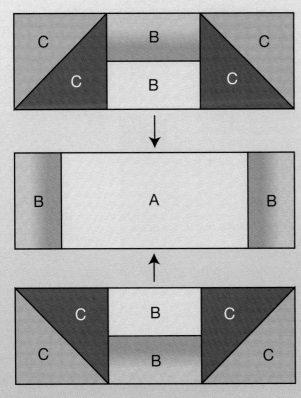

Figure 11. Block Assembly

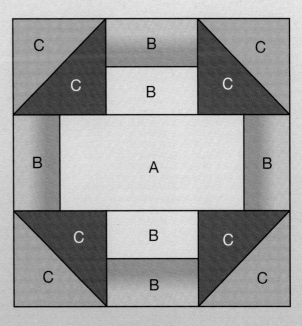

Calling Card

🎕 *Assembly* 🎕

1. Sign the A rectangle as desired, referring to Signature Methods on pages 12–15. Take care to stay inside the ¼" seam allowances.

2. Sew a gold-pink stripe B rectangle to each side of the A rectangle as shown (Fig. 7, page 31). Press the seam allowances toward the B rectangles.

3. With a pencil, mark a diagonal line on the wrong side of a gold C square. Place a gold C square and a pink C square right sides together. To make two half-square triangle units, sew ¼" away from the diagonal line on each side. Cut the units apart on the marked line. Repeat to make four half-square units. Press the seam allowances toward the gold triangles (Fig. 8).

4. Sew the two remaining gold-pink stripe B rectangles to the two pale yellow B rectangles as shown (Fig. 9). Press the seam allowances toward the gold-pink rectangles.

Detail of signature area in CALLING CARD, page 33

5. Sew the half-square triangle units from step 3 to the B/B units from step 4. Press the seam allowances toward the B/B units (Fig. 10, page 31).

6. Arrange three rows of units as shown and sew the rows togeth-

er (Fig. 11). Press the seam allowances toward the A rectangle to complete the block. Trim the seam allowance of the dark fabric to ⅛" if it shows through the light fabric.

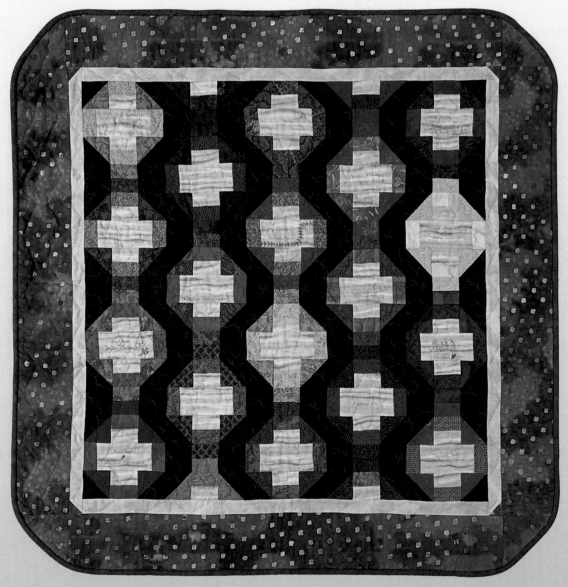

CALLING CARD, *40" x 40", assembled by the author. A former magazine editor gathered signatures from all the editors and assistants at the magazine and gave them to the author in 1996. The blocks were put together with pieced sashing and half blocks to produce the offset pattern.*

Crazy Friends

Finished Block Size: 4" x 4"

To showcase a wide variety of fabrics and colors, a crazy quilt format is a great choice for this Crazy Friends block. Additional embroidery or inked drawings would add to the nostalgic look.

❧ Cutting ❧

Fabric	Pieces
Tan	One 5½" x 5½" signature A square
Assorted coordinating prints	Four or five odd-shaped pieces

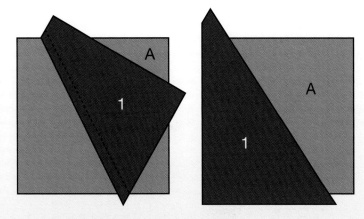

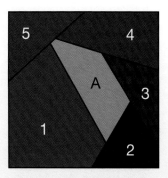

Figure 12. Sew piece #1 to the A foundation square and press.

Crazy Friends

◥◣ *Assembly* ◥◣

1. Sign the A square as desired, referring to Signature Methods on pages 12–15. Take care to allow space around your writing for the crazy patch pieces.

2. Use the A square as a foundation block for traditional crazy piecing. With right sides together, sew an odd-shaped piece onto the A square, making sure it is large enough to cover the edges of the foundation square when opened, and that the seam will not overlap the signature area. Open the first piece and press (Fig. 12). Trim the seam allowance to ¼" on the wrong side of the odd-shaped piece. Do not trim the foundation signature A square.

3. Referring to the block diagram as a guide, continue adding odd-shaped pieces to the A square as described in step 2 in a counterclockwise direction. Change the angles of the seams as desired.

4. When the A square is covered with patches, except for the signature area, trim the completed block to 4½" x 4½" square. You may also trim the excess foundation fabric, if desired.

Crazy Friends

CRAZY FRIENDS, *34" x 34"*, assembled by the author. At Quilt Colorado 1988, the author won fifty squares of rainbow-hued fabrics as a door prize. Friends and teachers signed the squares as a remembrance of the occasion. Using the squares as a foundation, she assembled blocks as a crazy quilt.

Detail of signature area in CRAZY FRIENDS

Finished Block Size: 10" x 10"

The Crossing Paths block offers an opportunity to use an interesting theme fabric. Choose one that relates to the recipient's interests.

ଓଚ Cutting ଚଓ

Fabric	Pieces
Yellow	Two 3½" x 3½" signature A squares
Teal	One 2½" x 2½" B square Four 2" x 2" E squares Four 1½" x 1½" F squares
Yellow theme print	Four 2½" x 4½" C rectangles
Stripe	Eight 1½" x 3½" D rectangles
Red	Four 2" x 2" E squares

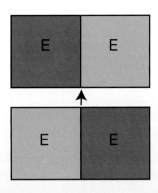

Figure 13. Sew the teal and red E squares together in pairs. Make two.

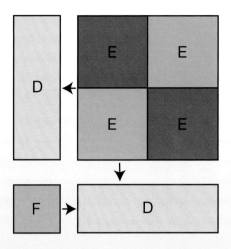

Figure 14. Unit 1 assembly, make two.

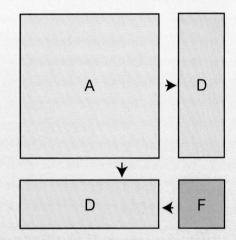

Figure 15. Unit 2 assembly, make two.

✂ *Assembly* ✂

1. Sign one or both of the A squares as desired, referring to Signature Methods on pages 12–15. Take care to stay inside the ¼" seam allowances.

2. Sew the teal and red E squares together in pairs. Press the seam allowances toward the teal squares. Sew two of these pairs together as shown. Press the seam allowance in the direction of the arrow. Make two of these units (Fig. 13).

3. Sew a stripe D rectangle to the unit from step 2. Press the seam allowance in the direction of the arrow. Sew a stripe D rectangle to a teal F square. Press. Sew these pieces together, as shown, completing Unit 1 (Fig. 14). Press. Make two of Unit 1.

4. Sew a stripe D rectangle to an A square as shown. Press the seam allowance in the direction of the arrow. Sew a stripe D rectangle to a teal F square. Press. Sew these pieces together as shown, completing Unit 2 (Fig. 15). Make two of Unit 2.

5. Sew units 1 and 2, four C rectangles, and the B square into rows as shown (Fig. 16). Press the seam allowances in the direction of the arrows. Sew the rows together to complete the block. Press.

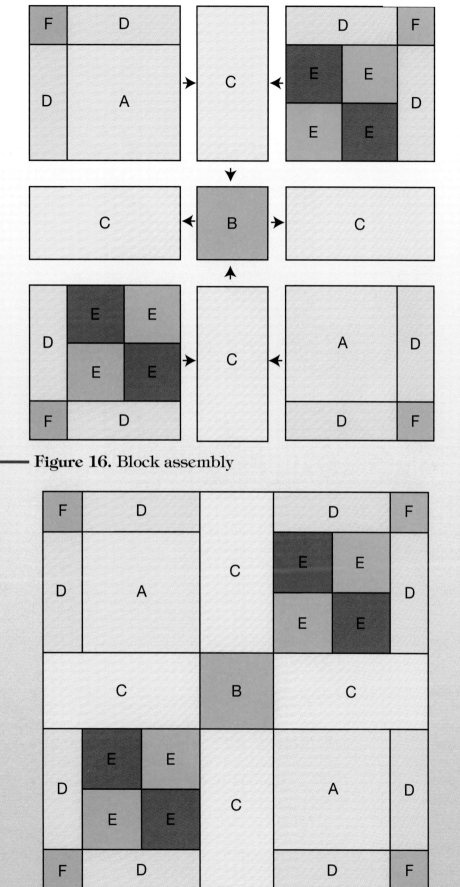

Figure 16. Block assembly

Crossing Paths

Daylight into Darkness

Finished Block Size: 6" x 6"

By choosing fabric values carefully, secondary patterns emerge when Daylight into Darkness is straight-set, without sashing.

❧❧ Cutting ❧❧

Fabric	Pieces
Light blue	Two 3½" x 1½" signature A rectangles One 4¼" x 4¼" square, cut in quarters diagonally, for four B triangles
Assorted dark blue	Four 3½" x 1½" A rectangles One 4¼" x 4¼" square, cut in quarters diagonally, for four B triangles

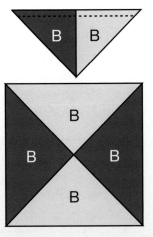

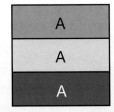

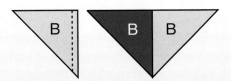

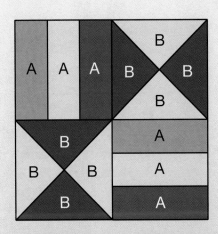

Figure 17. Unit 1 assembly, make two.

Figure 18. Sew the light blue and dark blue B triangles together to make four triangle units.

Figure 19. Unit 2 assembly, make two.

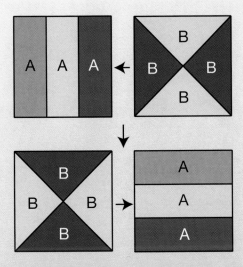

Figure 20. Block assembly

Daylight into Darkness

✂ *Assembly* ✂

1. Sign the two light blue A rectangles as desired, referring to Signature Methods on pages 12–15. Take care to stay inside the ¼" seam allowances.

2. Sew a dark blue A rectangle to each side of a signature A rectangle, completing Unit 1 (Fig. 17). Press the seam allowances toward the dark rectangles. Make two of Unit 1.

3. Right sides together, sew one light blue B triangle to a dark blue B triangle along one short side as shown (Fig. 18). Press the seam allowance toward the dark triangle. Make four of these triangle units.

Daylight into Darkness

4. Right sides together, sew two of the triangle units together along the long edge, completing Unit 2 (Fig. 19, page 41). Press. Make two of Unit 2.

5. Sew units 1 and 2 together as shown (Fig. 20). Press the seam allowances in the direction of the arrows. Sew the two rows together, completing the block.

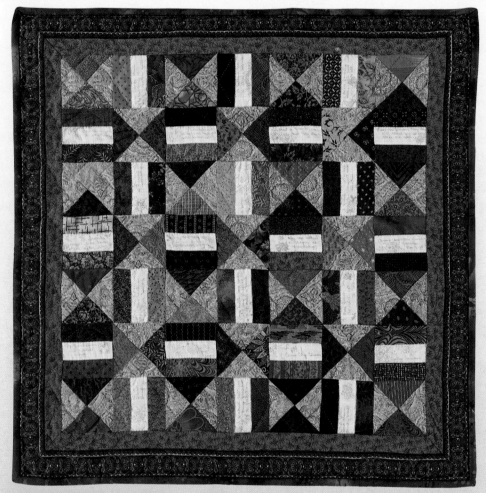

DAYLIGHT INTO DARKNESS, 27" x 27", made by the author. This quilt contains sentiments of friendship, such as "friendship introduces daylight into darkness."

Detail of signature area in DAYLIGHT INTO DARKNESS

Finished Block Size: 7½" x 7½"

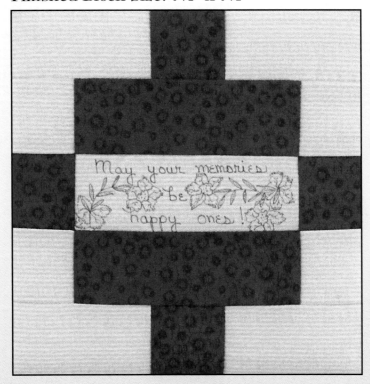

Reminiscent of the traditional Album Patch that was usually set on-point, this Deco Album block is an updated version for ease of construction.

❧ *Cutting* ❧

Fabric	Pieces
Gold print	One 2" x 5" signature A rectangle Four 2" x 2" B squares Four 2" x 3½" C rectangles
Red print	Two 2" x 5" A rectangles Four 2" x 2" B squares

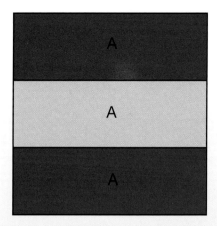

Figure 21. Unit 1 assembly, make one.

Figure 22. Unit 2 assembly, make two.

Figure 23. Unit 3 assembly, make two.

❦ Assembly ❦

1. Sign the gold A rectangle as desired, referring to Signature Methods on pages 12–15. Take care to stay inside the ¼" seam allowance.

2. Sew the red A rectangles to each long side of the gold A rectangle, completing Unit 1 (Fig. 21). Press the seam allowances toward the red rectangles.

3. Sew two gold B squares to opposite sides of a red B square, completing Unit 2 (Fig. 22). Press the seam allowances toward the red square. Make two of Unit 2.

4. Sew two gold C rectangles to each side of a red B square, completing Unit 3 (Fig. 23). Press the seam allowances toward the red square. Make two of Unit 3.

5. Sew Unit 2 to each side of Unit 1. Press the seam allowances in the direction of the arrows. Sew Unit 3 to the top and bottom of units 1 and 2, completing the block (Fig. 24, page 45). Press.

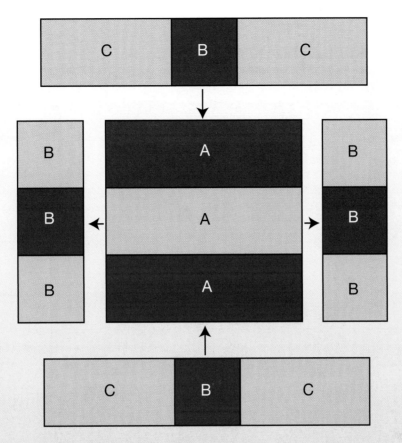

Figure 24. Block assembly

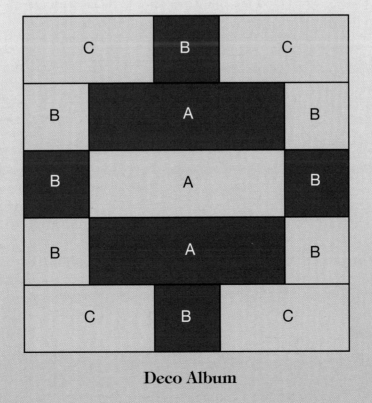

Deco Album

Dream West

Finished Block Size: 7½" x 7½"

For a traditional look, set the Dream West block in strippy style, with 3"-wide striped sashing. Frame the quilt with a nostalgic floral border.

🗝 Cutting 🗝

Fabric	Pieces
Beige	One 5" x 2" signature A rectangle
Dark red print	Two 5" x 2" A rectangles
Small blue print	Four 2" x 2" B squares
Medium red print	Two 5" x 2" A rectangles Two 8" x 2" C rectangles
Large blue print	Four 3½" x 3½" D squares

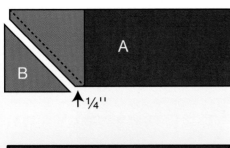

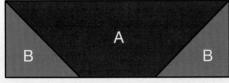

Figure 25. Unit 1 assembly, make two.

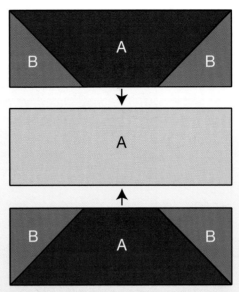

Figure 26. Sew Unit 1 to each long side of the beige signature A rectangle.

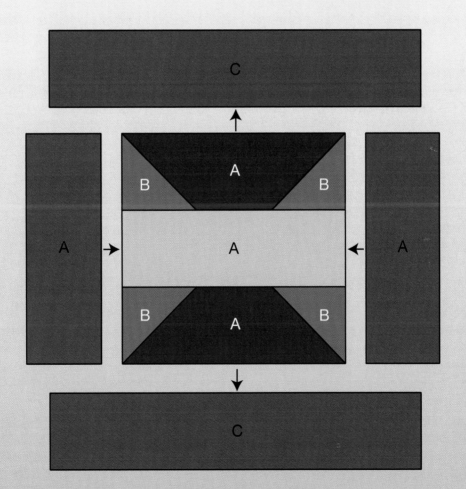

Figure 27. Sew the red A rectangles and the red C rectangles to the signature unit.

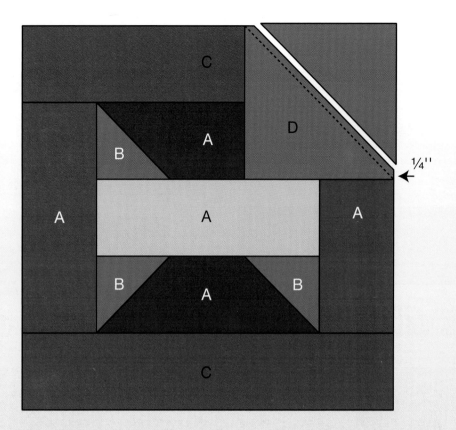

Figure 28. Sew a blue print D square in a corner of the unit.

❦ *Assembly* ❦

1. Sign the beige A rectangle as desired, referring to Signature Methods on pages 12–15. Take care to stay inside the ¼" seam allowances.

2. With a pencil, mark a diagonal line on the wrong side of the four blue B squares. Right sides together, place a marked B square on one end of a red print A rectangle. Sew on the marked line. Trim the seam allowance to ¼" and press it toward the B triangle. Repeat with another B square on the opposite end of the red print A rectangle, completing Unit 1 (Fig. 25, page 47). Press. Make two of Unit 1.

3. Sew Unit 1 to each long side of the beige A rectangle as shown, (Fig. 26). Press the seam allowance toward the beige A rectangle. Trim the seam allowance of the dark fabric to ⅛" if necessary.

4. Sew the two red A rectangles to the sides of the unit from step 3 as shown. Press the seam allowances in the direction of the arrows. Sew the two red C rectangles to the top and bottom of this unit. Press (Fig. 27, page 47).

5. With a pencil, mark a diagonal line on the wrong side of the four blue print D squares.

Right sides together, place a marked D square on one corner of the unit from step 4. Sew on the marked line. Trim the seam allowance to ¼" and press it toward the D triangle (Fig. 28, page 48).

6. Sew the remaining three D squares on the other three corners of the unit, completing the block. Press.

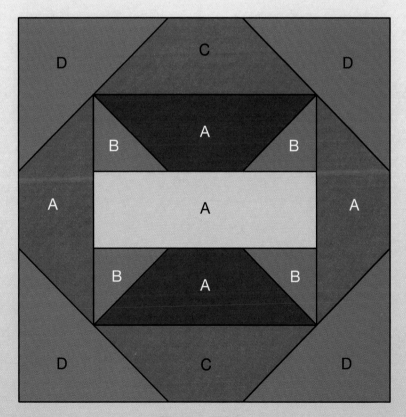

Dream West

Friends Together

Finished Block Size: 6" x 6"

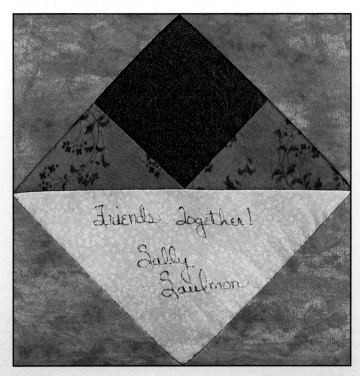

The triangular signature patch in Friends Together is ample in size to accommodate signatures and names of home towns, plus a drawing to personalize the block.

🕊 Cutting 🕊

Fabric	Pieces
Light green print	One 5⅛" x 5⅛" square, cut in half diagonally, for the signature A triangle
Medium red print	Two 3⅞" x 3⅞" squares, cut in half diagonally, for four B triangles
Dark red print	One 3" x 3" square, cut in half diagonally, for two C triangles
Dark green print	One 2⅝" x 2⅝" D square

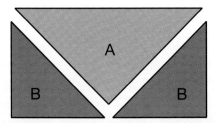

Figure 29. Unit 1 assembly, make one.

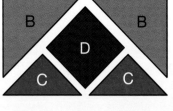

Figure 30. Unit 2 assembly, make one.

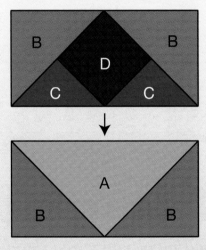

Figure 31. Block assembly

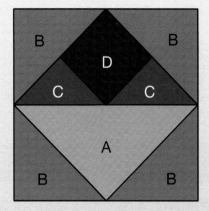

Friends Together

❧❧ *Assembly* ❧❧

1. Sign the A triangle as desired, referring to Signature Methods on pages 12–15. Take care to stay inside the ¼" seam allowances.

2. Sew a medium red B triangle to each short edge of the A triangle, completing Unit 1 (Fig. 29). Press the seam allowances toward the B triangles.

3. Sew a dark red C triangle to two adjoining sides of the D square, forming a triangle. Press the seam allowances toward the C triangles. Sew the two remaining medium red B triangles to the pieced triangle as shown, completing Unit 2 (Fig. 30). Press the seam allowances toward the B triangles.

4. Sew units 1 and 2 together to complete the block (Fig. 31). Press the seam allowances toward the A triangle.

Friends Together

FRIENDS TOGETHER, *49" x 37", made and hand quilted by the author. Sally designed the Friends Together block specifically for a block drawing held during the Quilt Colorado 1992 symposium, sponsored by the Colorado Quilting Council. The committee chairpeople exchanged blocks that resulted in this strippy-style quilt. Jane Doak designed the symposium logo block in the lower right corner.*

Detail of signature area in FRIENDS TOGETHER

Golden Moments

Finished Block Size: 7" x 7"

When set on-point, the Golden Moments block can be quite sophisticated, especially when an unusual fabric is chosen for the B pieces.

✂ Cutting ✂

Fabric	Pieces
Light yellow print	One 3½" x 3½" signature A square
Blue and white print	Four 3½" x 2½" B rectangles
Dark blue print	Twelve 1½" x 1½" C squares Two 2⅞" x 2⅞" D squares
Medium yellow print	Two 2⅞" x 2⅞" D squares

Golden Moments

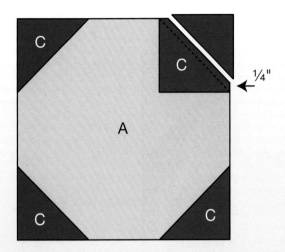

Figure 32. Unit 1 assembly, make one.

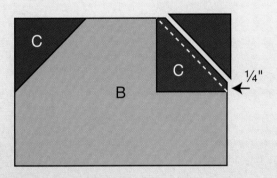

Figure 33. Unit 2 assembly, make four.

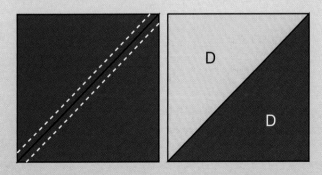

Figure 34. Unit 3 assembly, make four.

✺ Assembly ✺

1. With a pencil, mark a diagonal line on the wrong side of the twelve dark blue C squares. Right sides together, place a C square on one corner of the A square. Sew on the marked line. Trim the seam allowance to ¼" and press it toward the blue triangle. Repeat for the other three corners of the A square, completing Unit 1 (Fig. 32).

2. Sign the A area in Unit 1 as desired, referring to Signature Methods on pages 12–15. Take care to stay inside the ¼" seam allowances.

3. Right sides together, place a dark blue C square in one corner of a blue and white B rectangle. Sew on the marked line. Trim the seam allowance to ¼" and press it toward the blue triangle. Sew another dark blue C square at the opposite corner as shown, completing Unit 2. Make four of Unit 2 (Fig. 33).

4. With a pencil, mark a diagonal line on the wrong side of the two medium yellow print D squares. Place one yellow print D square and one dark blue D square right sides together. To make two half-square units, sew ¼" away from the diagonal line on each side. Cut the units apart on the marked line. Repeat to make four half-square triangles, completing Unit 3 (Fig. 34). Press the seam allowances toward the blue triangles.

5. Sew units 1, 2, and 3 into rows as shown (Fig. 35). Press the seam allowances in the direction of the arrows. Sew the rows together, completing the block. Press.

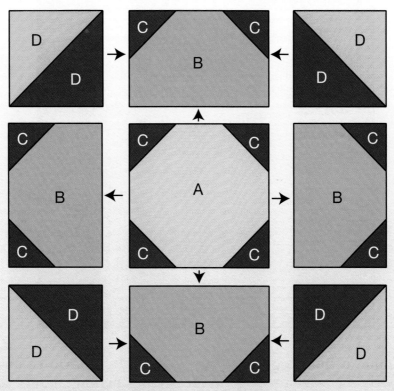

Figure 35. Block assembly

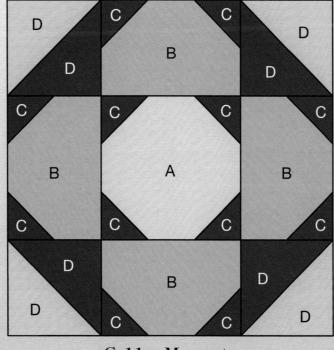

Golden Moments

Happy the Home

Finished Block Size: 6" x 6"

Happy the Home, a half Log Cabin block, has the charm of an old favorite. Experiment with the various Log Cabin setting arrangements for surprising results.

➷ Cutting ➹

Fabric	Pieces
Light green print	One 3½" x 3½" signature A square
Assorted green prints	One 1½" x 3½" rectangle (piece 1) One 1½" x 4½" rectangle (piece 3) One 1½" x 5½" rectangle (piece 5)
Assorted rust prints	One 1½" x 4½" rectangle (piece 2) One 1½" x 5½" rectangle (piece 4) One 1½" x 6½" rectangle (piece 6)

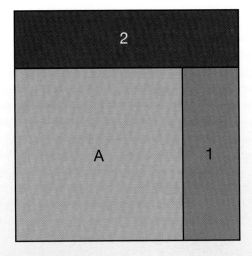

Figure 36. Sew green piece 1
and rust piece 2 to the A
square.

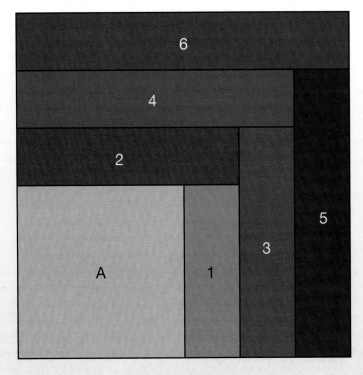

Happy the Home

❦ *Assembly* ❦

1. Sign the A square as desired,
   referring to Signature Methods
   on pages 12–15. Take care to
   stay inside the ¼" seam
   allowances.

2. Sew green piece 1 to the side of
   the A square as shown. Press
   the seam allowance toward
   piece 1. Sew rust piece 2 to the
   top of the A square as shown
   (Fig. 36). Press the seam
   allowance toward piece 2.

3. Continue to add pieces 3
   through 6 in the same manner,
   completing the block. Press all
   seam allowances away from the
   A square.

Happy the
Home

HAPPY THE HOME, *47" x 47",*
made by the author. The signa-
ture squares in this quilt feature
drawings and sentiments of
home, all hand-inked by the
author. The blocks are rotated to
produce a diagonal pattern.

Detail of signature area in
HAPPY THE HOME

SUNSHINE AND SHADOW, *41" x
41", assembled and hand quilted
by the author. The Happy the
Home blocks in this quilt were
made, signed, and exchanged by
the chairpeople of Quilt Colorado
2000. The author assembled the
blocks with sashing and pieced
cornerstone blocks.*

Detail of signature area in SUN-
SHINE AND SHADOW

Keepsake Star

Finished Block Size: 7½" x 7½"

It is fun to carry 3-inch squares of fabric when you travel, and ask people you meet along the way to sign them. Use this Keepsake Star block to collect signatures and create a quilt that is a remembrance of a special trip.

❧❧ Cutting ❧❧

Fabric	Pieces
White print	One 3" x 3" signature A square Eight 1¾" x 1¾" B squares
Green print	Four 1¾" x 3" C rectangles Four 1¾" x 1¾" D squares
Blue-green polka dot	Four 1¾" x 1¾" D squares
Blue-green print	Four 5½" x 1¾" E rectangles

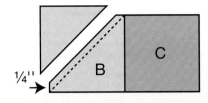
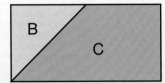

Figure 37. Sew a marked B square on one side of a green C rectangle.

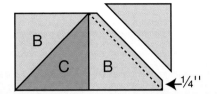
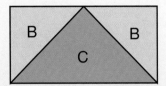

Figure 38. Star-point unit, make four.

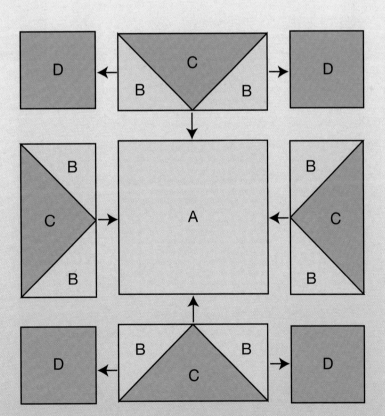

Figure 39. Star unit assembly, make one.

Keepsake Star

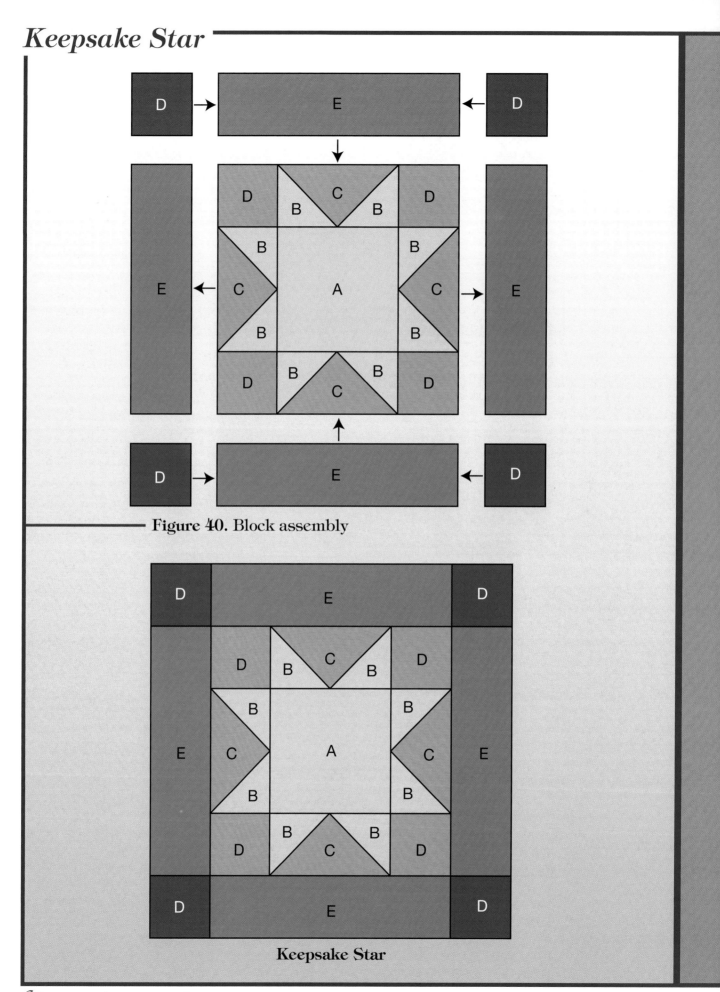

Figure 40. Block assembly

Keepsake Star

❦ Assembly ❦

1. Sign the A square as desired, referring to Signature Methods on pages 12–15. Take care to stay inside the ¼" seam allowances.

2. With a pencil, mark a diagonal line on the wrong side of the eight white B squares. Right sides together, place a marked white B square on one side of a green C rectangle. Sew on the marked line. Trim the seam allowance to ¼" (Fig. 37, page 61). Open and press the seam allowance toward the white triangle. Trim the seam allowance of the dark fabric to ⅛" if necessary.

3. Repeat step 2 with another white B square at the opposite side of the same C rectangle, completing the star-point unit (Fig. 38). Make four star-point units.

4. Sew two green D squares to a star-point unit. Repeat, reversing the direction of the star-point unit. Sew a star-point unit to each side of the white A square. Press the seam allowances in the direction of the arrows. Sew the three rows together, completing the star unit (Fig. 39). Press the seam allowances toward the middle row.

5. Sew two polka dot D squares to the short sides of a blue-green print E rectangle. Repeat. Sew two E rectangles to the sides of the star unit. Press the seam allowances in the direction of the arrows. Sew the rows together, completing the block (Fig. 40, page 62). Press the seam allowances toward the middle row.

Keepsake Star

KEEPSAKE STAR, *38" x 38",
made by the author. Students
on the author's teaching trip
to Michigan signed the signature squares, and the author
did the drawings. The blocks
were set with a pieced sashing
to provide even more signature squares in the design.

**Detail of signature area in
KEEPSAKE STAR**

Finished Block Size: 8" x 8"

For a dynamic quilt containing the Legacy block, combine shaded, hand-dyed, or batik fabrics with an innovative setting or pieced sashing.

∞ Cutting ∞

Fabric	Pieces
Light blue print	One 4⅞" x 4⅞" square, cut in half diagonally, for two signature A triangles Two of Template B
Medium blue print	One 4⅞" x 4⅞" square, cut in half diagonally, for two A triangles Two of Template B
Brown print	One 5¼" x 5¼" square, cut in quarters diagonally, for four C triangles
Rust print	One 3¼" x 3¼" square, cut in quarters diagonally, for four D triangles Four 2½" x 2½" E squares

Template is on page 68.

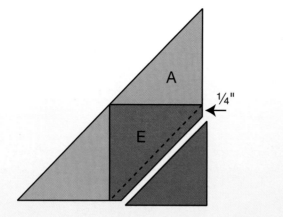
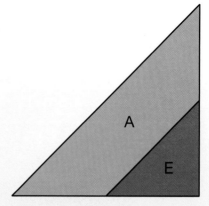

Figure 41. Light blue/rust Unit 1 assembly, make two.

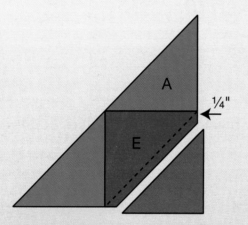
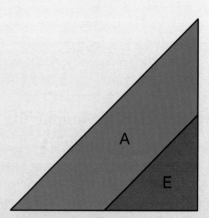

Figure 42. Medium blue/rust Unit 1 assembly, make two.

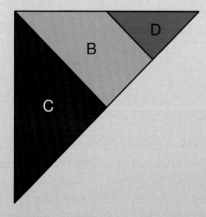
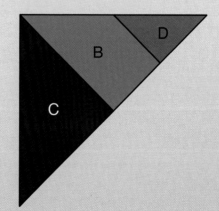

Figure 43. Brown/light blue/rust Unit 2 assembly, make two.

Figure 44. Brown/medium blue/rust Unit 2 assembly, make two.

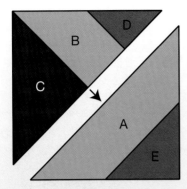

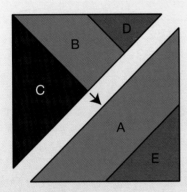

Figure 45. Sew units 1 and 2 together.

❦ *Assembly* ❦

1. With a pencil, mark a diagonal line on the wrong side of the four rust E squares. Right sides together, place the corner of a marked E square on the tip of a light blue A triangle. Sew on the marked line. Trim the seam allowance to ¼" and press it toward the rust triangle, completing Unit 1 (Fig. 41, page 66). Make two of the light blue/rust Unit 1.

2. Repeat step 1 to make two more of Unit 1, this time with two medium blue A triangles and two rust E squares (Fig. 42).

3. Sign one or both of the light blue A triangles as desired, referring to Signature Methods on pages 12–15. Take care to stay inside the ¼" seam allowances.

4. Right sides together, sew a light blue B piece to a brown C triangle as shown. Press the seam allowance toward the brown triangle. Sew a rust D triangle to the opposite side of the B piece, completing Unit 2 (Fig. 43). Press. Make two of the brown/light blue/rust Unit 2.

5. Repeat step 4 to make two more of Unit 2, this time with two brown C triangles, two medium blue B pieces, and two rust D triangles (Fig. 44).

6. Sew units 1 and 2 together as shown, placing the light blue units together and the medium blue units together. Press the seam allowances toward Unit 1 (Fig. 45).

7. Sew a medium blue unit to a light blue unit as shown. Press the seam allowances toward the medium blue unit. Repeat with the other light blue and medium blue units. Sew the two rows of units together, completing the block (Fig. 46, page 68). Press.

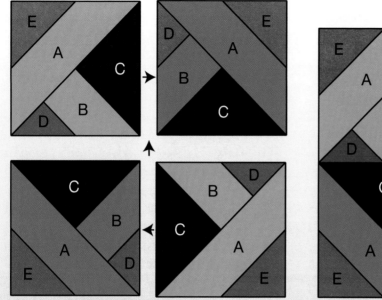

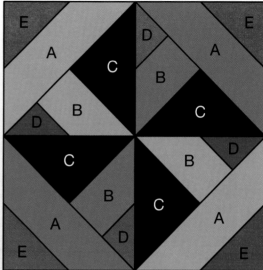

Figure 46. Block assembly

Legacy

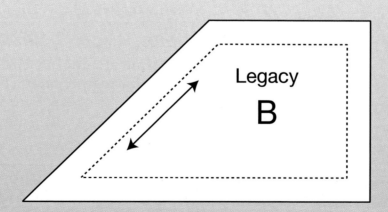

Legacy
B

Finished Block Size: 6" x 6"

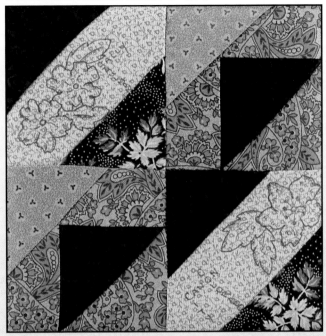

You can create a dynamic quilt by controlling the values of the colors you use in each Migration block. Use a striped border fabric in complementary colors to frame the blocks.

⚙ Cutting ⚙

Fabric	Pieces
Pale pink print	Two 3½" x 3½" signature A squares
Burgundy print	Two 2½" x 2½" B squares One 2⅞" x 2⅞" C square
Green and burgundy print	Two 2½" x 2½" B squares
Pink print	One 2⅞" x 2⅞" C square Two 1½" x 2½" D rectangles Two 1½" x 3½" E rectangles
Green print	Two 2½" x 2½" B squares

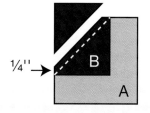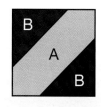

¼"→

Figure 47. Unit 1 assembly, make two.

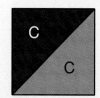

Figure 48. Half-square triangle units, make two.

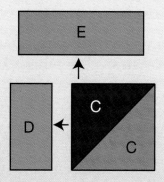

Figure 49. Sew a pink D and a pink E rectangle to the half-square triangle unit.

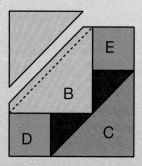

Figure 50. Unit 2 assembly, make two.

❧ Assembly ❧

1. With a pencil, mark a diagonal line on the wrong side of each B square. Right sides together, place a marked burgundy B square on the top left corner of a pale pink A square. Sew on the marked line. Trim the seam allowance to ¼". Open and press the seam allowance toward the B triangle. Sew a green and burgundy B square to the opposite corner of the A square, completing Unit 1 (Fig. 47). Press the seam allowance toward the B triangle. Make two of Unit 1.

2. Sign the A area of Unit 1 as desired, referring to Signature Methods on pages 12–15.

3. With a pencil, mark a diagonal line on the wrong side of the pink C square. Right sides together, place the marked C square on a burgundy C square. Sew a ¼" seam on both sides of the marked line. Cut along the marked line to create two half-square triangle units (Fig. 48). Press the seam allowances toward the dark triangles.

4. Sew a pink D rectangle to the burgundy side of a half-square triangle unit. Press the seam allowance toward the D rectangle. Sew a pink E rectangle to the top edge of this unit. Press the seam allowance toward the E rectangle. Repeat with the other half-square triangle unit and pink rectangles (Fig. 49).

5. With a pencil, mark a diagonal line on the wrong side of two green print B squares. Right sides together, place a marked B square in the top left corner of a unit from step 4. Sew on the marked line and trim the seam allowance to ¼", completing Unit 2 (Fig. 50, page 70). Press the seam allowance toward the B triangle. Make two of Unit 2.

6. Sew units 1 and 2 together as shown. Press the seam allowances in the direction of the arrows. Sew the two rows together, completing the block (Fig. 51).

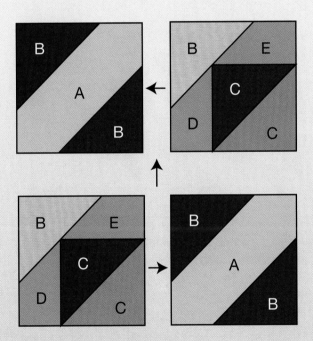

Figure 51. Block assembly

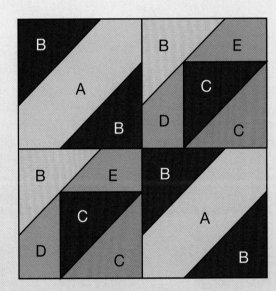

Migration

Migration

MIGRATION, *30" x 30", made by the author. The blocks in this quilt were signed at a Colorado Quilting Council retreat to commemorate the event.*

Detail of signature area in MIGRATION

Mountain Memories

Finished Block Size: 6" x 6"

Six-inch square blocks are a good size to use for block drawings. You can make a nice wall quilt with twenty-four Mountain Memories blocks set on point.

❧ Cutting ❧

Fabric	Pieces
Light blue print	One 9¾" x 2⅝" signature A rectangle
Purple print	One 3⅞" x 3⅞" square, cut in half diagonally, for two B triangles
Light print	Two 3⅞" x 3⅞" squares, cut in half diagonally, for three B triangles

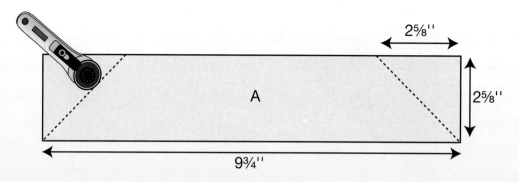

Figure 52. Create a trapezoid from the A rectangle.

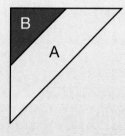

Figure 53. Unit 1 assembly, make one.

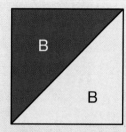

Figure 54. Sew the purple B triangle to the light print B triangle.

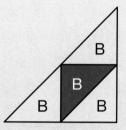

Figure 55. Unit 2 assembly, make one.

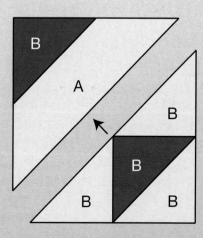

Figure 56. Block assembly

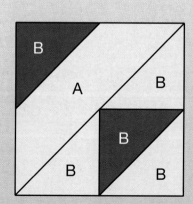

Mountain Memories

✣ Assembly ✣

1. Cut each end of the 9¾" x 2⅝" light blue A rectangle at a 45–degree angle to create a trapezoid (Fig. 52, page 74). Sign the A trapezoid as desired, referring to Signature Methods on pages 12–15. Take care to stay inside the ¼" seam allowances.

2. Sew a purple print B triangle to the light blue A trapezoid, as shown. Press the seam allowance toward the B triangle, completing Unit 1 (Fig. 53).

3. Sew the remaining purple B triangle to the light print B triangle to form a square. Press the seam allowance toward the purple triangle (Fig. 54).

4. Sew the remaining two light print B triangles to the square from step 3. Press the seam allowances toward the light print triangles, completing Unit 2 (Fig. 55).

5. Sew units 1 and 2 together to complete the block (Fig. 56). Press the seam allowance toward the A piece.

Detail of signature area in MOUNTAIN MEMORIES, page 76

Mountain
Memories

MOUNTAIN MEMORIES, *48" x 48", assembled and hand quilted by the author. The committee chairpeople of the Quilt Colorado 1994 symposium exchanged in friendship the Mountain Memories block. The author assembled her blocks on-point with a striped sashing to unify the blocks.*

Finished Block Size: 6" x 9"

Have the center rectangle pieces available at a high school graduation party for everyone to inscribe sentiments and their signatures. Complete the quilt in the recipient's favorite colors for a quilt that would brighten any dormitory room with fond memories.

❧ Cutting ❧

Fabric	Pieces
Light print	One 6½" x 3½" signature A rectangle
Dark print	Two 4¼" x 4¼" squares, cut in quarters diagonally, for six B triangles
Medium print	One 4¼" x 4¼" square, cut in quarters diagonally, for two B triangles Two 3⅞" x 3⅞" squares, cut in half diagonally, for four C triangles

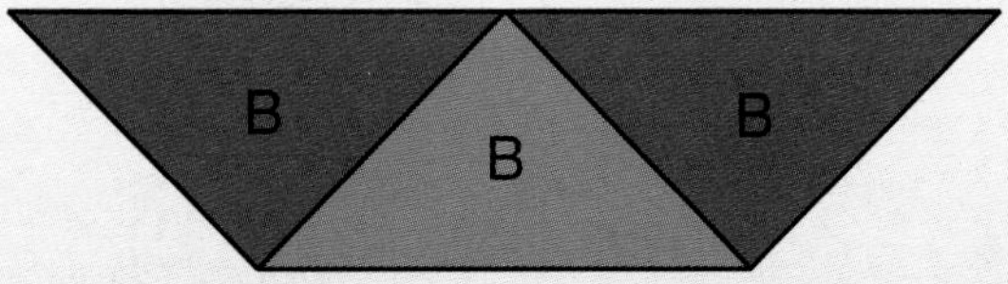

Figure 57. Unit 1 assembly, make two.

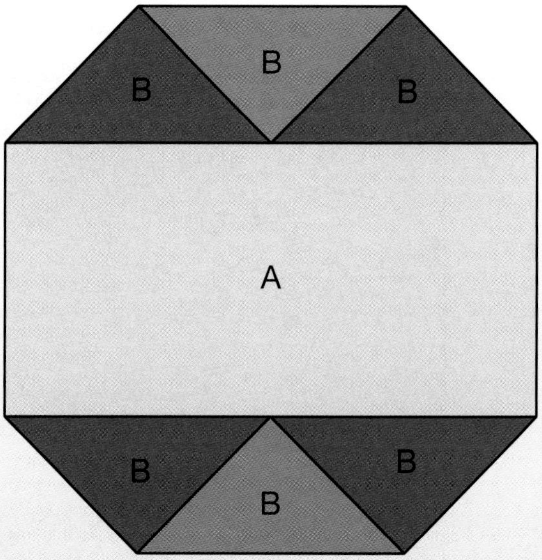

Figure 58. Sew Unit 1 to opposite edges of the A rectangle.

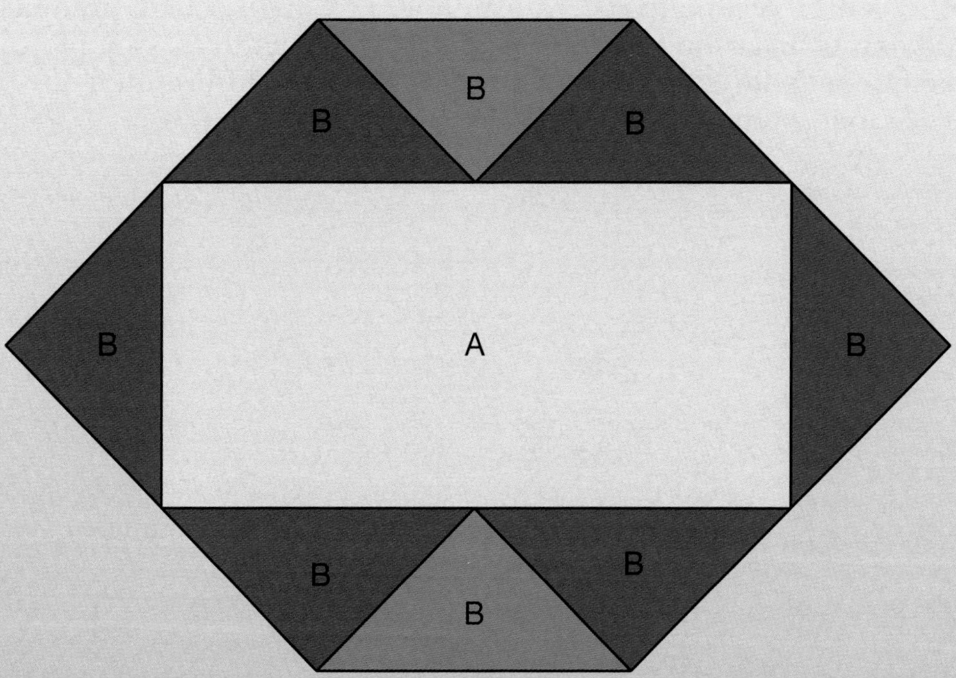

Figure 59. Sew a dark B triangle to each short edge of the unit.

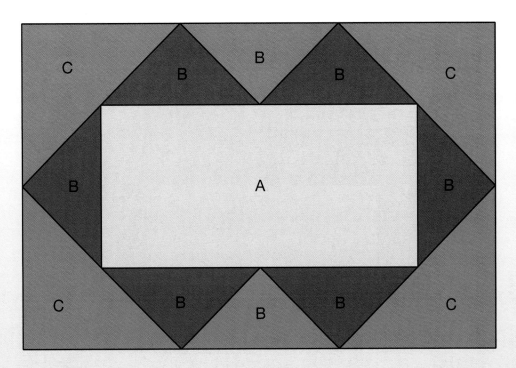

Places to Go

✸ *Assembly* ✸

1. Sign the A rectangle as desired, referring to Signature Methods on pages 12–15. Take care to stay inside the ¼" seam allowances.

2. Sew a medium B triangle between two dark B triangles along the short sides as shown (Fig. 57), page 78. Press the seam allowances toward the dark triangles, completing Unit 1. Make two of Unit 1.

3. Sew Unit 1 to the long edge of the A rectangle. Press the seam allowance toward the A rectangle. Sew another Unit 1 to the opposite edge of the A rectangle (Fig. 58). Press.

4. Sew the remaining two dark B triangles to the short edges of the unit from step 3 (Fig. 59). Press the seam allowances toward the dark triangles.

5. Sew the four medium C triangles to each corner of the unit, completing the block. Press the seam allowances toward the C triangles.

Quilting Connection

Finished Block Size: 6" x 8"

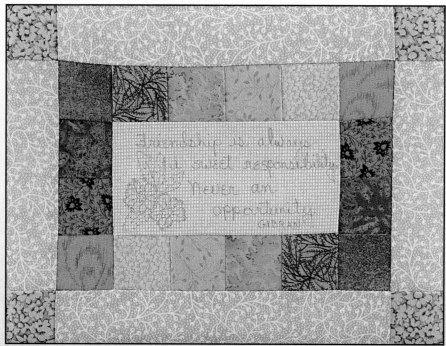

Quilting Connection requires signature patches of 4½" x 2½", a natural size for signatures or sentiments.

❧❧ Cutting ❧❧

Fabric	Pieces
Light gold print	One 4½" x 2½" signature A rectangle
Assorted teal prints	Twenty 1½" x 1½" B squares
Medium gold print	Two 6½" x 1½" C rectangles Two 4½" x 1½" D rectangles

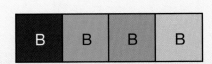

Figure 60. Make four B strips.

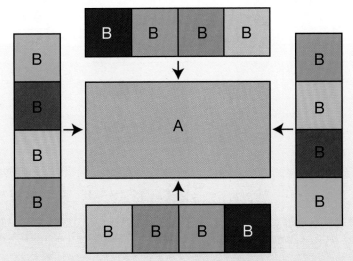

Figure 61. Sew a B strip to the edges of the A rectangle.

❧ *Assembly* ☙

1. Sign the A rectangle as desired, referring to Signature Methods on pages 12–15. Take care to stay inside the ¼" seam allowances.

2. Sew four teal B squares together to make a strip. Press the seam allowances the same direction. Make four B strips (Fig. 60).

3. Sew a B strip to each long edge of the A rectangle. Press the seam allowances toward the A rectangle. Sew a B strip to the remaining sides of this unit. Press, trimming the seam allowance of the dark fabric to ⅛" if necessary (Fig. 61).

4. Sew a B square to the short edges of two D rectangles as shown (Fig. 62, page 82). Press the seam allowances toward the D rectangles. Sew a medium gold C rectangle to the top and bottom edges of the signature unit. Press. Sew the B/D/B units to the sides of the signature unit, completing the block.

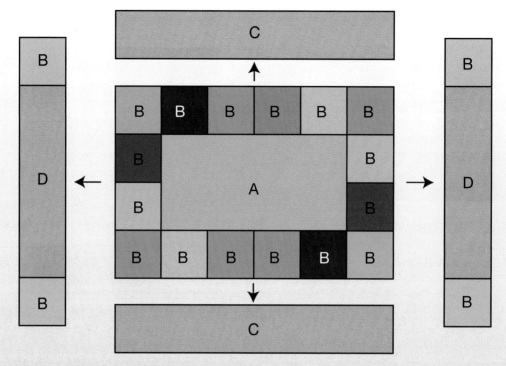

Figure 62. Block assembly

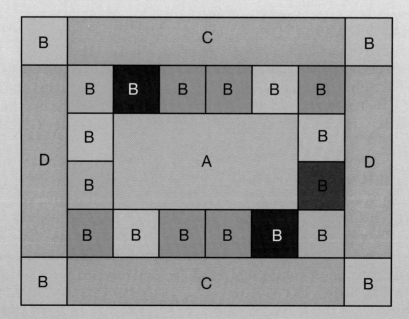

Quilting Connection

QUILTING CONNECTION, *65" x 52",
assembled and hand quilted by the
author. The committee chairpeople
of the Quilt Colorado 1998 symposium exchanged Quilting Connection blocks. The author assembled
her blocks with sashing and a
pieced border.*

Detail of signature area in QUILT-
ING CONNECTION

Quilting Connection

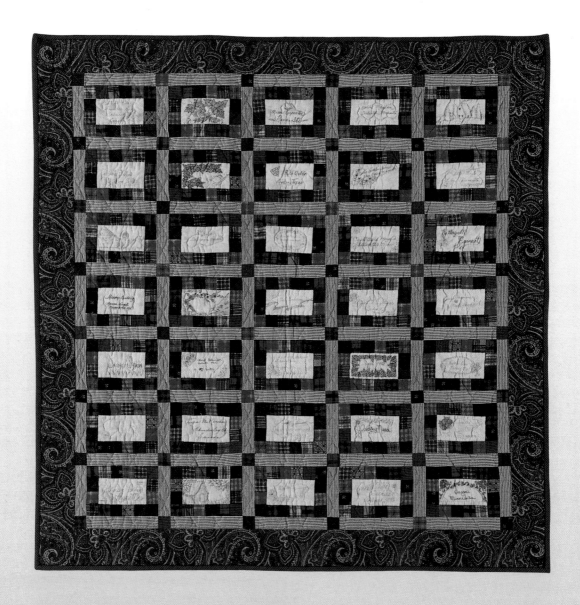

NEW FACES, NEW PLACES, *42" x 42", made by the author. Students in a Minnesota friendship quilt class signed the signature blocks in this quilt.*

Detail of signature area in NEW FACES, NEW PLACES

Finished Block Size: 9" x 9"

This Rising Star design is based on tradition. Use striped fabric to add movement to a quilt with offset blocks.

🕸 Cutting 🕸

Fabric	Pieces
Beige print	Two 3½" x 3½" signature A squares Four of Template F Four of Template Fr Four 2½" x 2½" H squares
Red print	One 3½" x 3½" B square Four 2⅜" x 2⅜" squares, cut in half diagonally, for eight D triangles
Blue print	Four 2" x 2" C squares Four of Template E
Stripe	Two 3½" x 3½" G squares

Templates are on page 87. A lowercase "r" indicates that a template should be reversed.

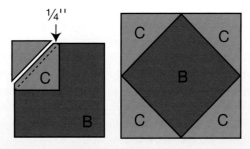

Figure 63. Unit 1 assembly, make one.

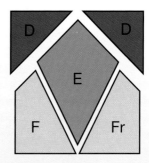

Figure 64. Unit 2 assembly, make four.

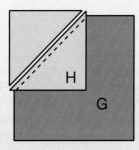
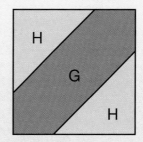

Figure 65. Unit 3 assembly, make two.

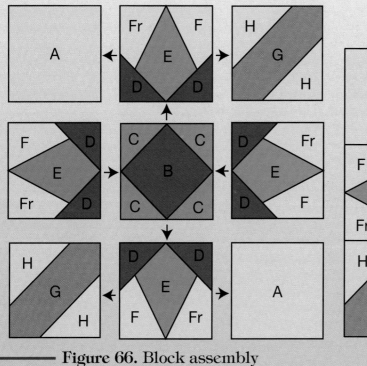

Figure 66. Block assembly

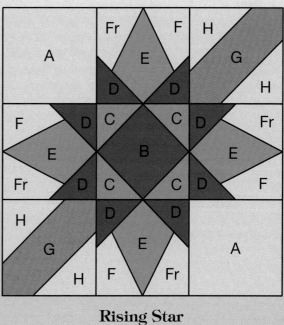

Rising Star

৩৫ Assembly ৩৫

1. Sign the two A squares as desired, referring to Signature Methods on pages 12–15. Take care to stay inside the ¼" seam allowances.

2. With a pencil, mark a diagonal line on the wrong side of the four blue C squares. Right sides together, place a marked C square on a corner of the red B square. Sew on the marked line. Trim the seam allowance to ¼". Repeat with the remaining three blue C squares in each corner of the B square, completing Unit 1 (Fig. 63, page 86). Press the seam allowances toward the C triangles.

3. Sew a beige F and Fr piece to each side of a blue E piece. Press the seam allowances toward the F pieces. Sew two red D triangles to this unit, completing Unit 2 (Fig. 64). Make four of this unit.

4. With a pencil, mark a diagonal line on the wrong side of the four beige H squares. Right sides together, place a marked H square in the top left corner of a striped G square. Sew on the marked line. Trim the seam allowance to ¼". Open and press the seam allowance toward the H triangle. Sew a beige H square at the bottom right corner of the unit, completing Unit 3 (Fig. 65). Press. Make two of this unit.

5. Sew the two A squares and units 1, 2, and 3 into rows as shown (Fig. 66). Press the seam allowances in the direction of the arrows. Sew the rows together, completing the block.

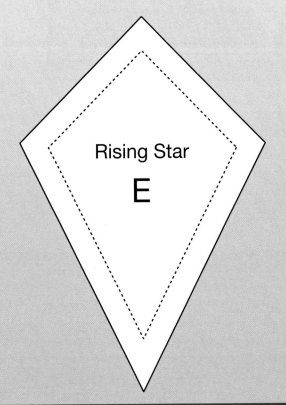

Rising Star

E

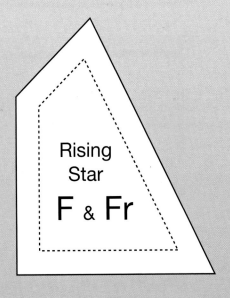

Rising Star

F & Fr

Rising Star

RISING STAR, 59" x 59", *made by the author. A sentiment about success by Ralph Waldo Emerson is inked on the Rising Star blocks in this quilt, which commemorates family college graduations. The stars appear to float and rise in this staggered setting.*

Detail of signature area in RISING STAR

Finished Block Size: 6" x 6"

HAPPINESS IS
NOT HAVING WHAT
YOU WANT, BUT WANTING
WHAT YOU HAVE.

Mother

When the Sunrise, Sunset block is rotated and straight-set without sashing, interesting secondary patterns evolve.

∞ Cutting ∞

Fabric	Pieces
Green print	One 7¼" x 7¼" square, cut in quarters diagonally, for one signature A triangle One 4¼" x 4¼" square, cut in quarters diagonally, for two B triangles
Orange print	One 4¼" x 4¼" square, cut in quarters diagonally, for two B triangles
Black print	One 2⅝" x 2⅝" C square
Stripe	One of Template D One of Template Dr

Template is on page 91. A lowercase "r" indicates that a template should be reversed.

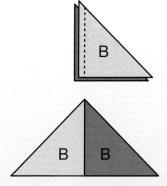

Figure 67. Unit 1 assembly, make one.

Figure 68. Unit 2 assembly, make one.

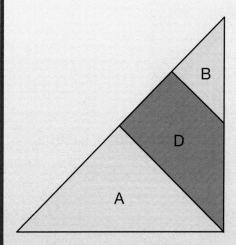

Figure 69. Unit 3 assembly, make one.

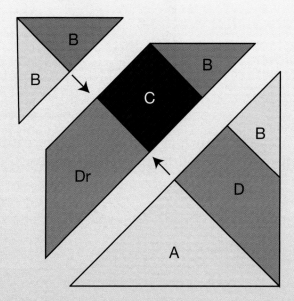

Figure 70. Block assembly

❧❧ *Assembly* ❧❧

1. Sew a green B triangle to an orange B triangle as shown, completing Unit 1 (Fig. 67). Press the seam allowance toward the orange triangle.

2. Sew the striped Dr piece to the black C square as shown. Press the seam allowance toward the striped piece. Sew an orange B triangle to the opposite side of the black C square, completing Unit 2 (Fig. 68). Press the seam allowance toward the orange triangle.

3. Sew the green A triangle to the striped D piece as shown. Press

the seam allowance toward the striped piece. Sew a green B triangle to the opposite side of the striped D piece as shown, completing Unit 3 (Fig. 69, page 90). Press the seam allowance toward the striped piece.

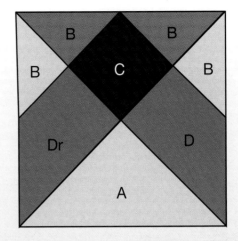

Sunrise, Sunset

4. Sew units 1, 2, and 3 together as shown, completing the block (Fig. 70). Press the seam allowances in the direction of the arrows.

5. Sign the A triangle as desired, referring to Signature Methods on pages 12–15.

Sunrise, Sunset

D & Dr

Tie that Binds

Finished Size for Blocks 1 and 2: 10" x 5"

Setting Tie that Binds blocks side by side in a quilt creates the look of a built-in sashing. The signature patch is large enough to accommodate genealogical information.

❧ Cutting ❧

Fabric	Pieces
Beige print	Two 4¼" x 4¼" signature A squares
Assorted red, blue, and brown prints	Four 3" x 3" B squares Six 1¾" x 1¾" D squares
Stripe	Four 1¾" x 3" C rectangles

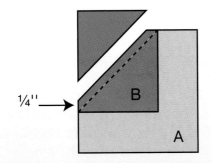
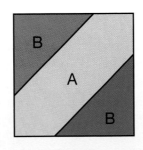

Figure 71. Unit 1 assembly, make two.

Figure 72. Unit 2 assembly, make four.

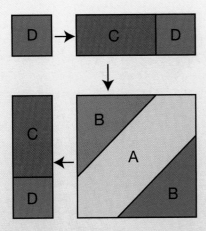
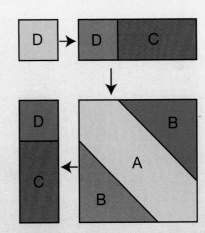

Figure 73. Block 1 assembly

Figure 74. Block 2 assembly

❧ Assembly ❧

1. With a pencil, mark a diagonal line on the wrong side of the four red, blue, or brown B squares. Right sides together, place a marked B square in the top left corner of a beige A square. Sew on the marked line. Trim the seam allowance to ¼". Open and press the seam allowance toward the B triangle. Sew another red, blue, or brown B square to the opposite corner of the square, completing Unit 1 (Fig. 71). Press the seam allowance toward the B triangle. Make two of Unit 1.

2. Sign the A area of Unit 1 as desired, referring to Signature Methods on pages 12–15.

3. Sew a red, blue, or brown D square to the short edge of a striped C rectangle, completing Unit 2 (Fig. 72). Press the seam allowance toward the D square. Make four of Unit 2.

4. Sew a blue D square, Unit 1, and two of Unit 2 together, as shown, completing Block 1 (Fig. 73, page 93). Press the seam allowances in the direction of the arrows.

5. Sew a brown D square, Unit 1, and two of Unit 2, alternating the direction of the signature area as shown, completing Block 2 (Fig. 74). Press the seam allowances in the direction of the arrows. Sew blocks 1 and 2 together as shown in the completed block diagram below.

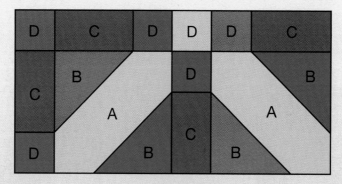

Tie that Binds

Detail of signature area in TIE THAT BINDS, *page 95*

TIE THAT BINDS, *36" x 36", made by the author. This quilt has six generations of genealogical information hand-inked on the signature blocks.*

Time Woven In

Finished Size for Blocks 1 and 2: 10" x 5"

By alternating the number of light and dark fabrics in two Time Woven In blocks and setting them on-point in a quilt, a woven pattern emerges.

⛤ Cutting ⛤

Fabric	Pieces
Assorted beige prints	Five 1½" x 5½" rectangles (at least one suitable for signature)
Assorted black and rust prints	Five 1½" x 5½" rectangles

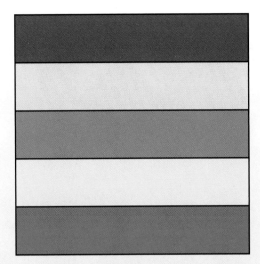

Figure 75. Block 1 assembly

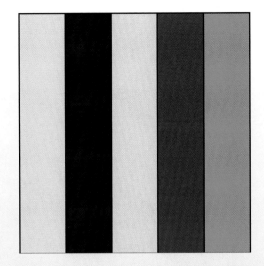

Figure 76. Block 2 assembly

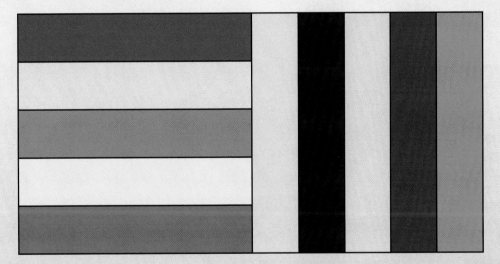

Time Woven In

⊱ Assembly ⊰

1. Sign the beige rectangle, as desired, referring to Signature Methods on pages 12–15. Take care to stay inside the ¼" seam allowances.

2. Sew two beige and three rust rectangles together, as shown, completing Block 1 (Fig. 75).

Press the seam allowances toward the rust rectangles.

3. Sew three beige and two black rectangles together, as shown, completing Block 2 (Fig. 76). Press the seam allowances toward the black rectangles.

Time Woven In

TIME WOVEN IN, *39" x 39", made by the author. The Time Woven In blocks were set on-point with setting triangles. Friends commemorated a class reunion by signing the quilt.*

Detail of signature area in TIME WOVEN IN

Tulip Time

Finished Block Size: 8" x 8"

Tulip Time is a design with plenty of space for signatures, sentiments, or drawings. With this block, you can create a contemporary or nostalgic look, depending on the fabrics you choose.

Cutting

Fabric	Pieces
Blue print	One 4½" x 4½" signature A square One 2⅞" x 2⅞" square, cut in half diagonally, for two C triangles One 1½" x 1½" D square One 1½" x 2½" E rectangle Two 2½" x 2½" F squares Two 2½" x 4½" G rectangles One 2½" x 2½" H square
Red print #1	One 4½" x 2½" B rectangle
Red print #2	One 2⅞" x 2⅞" square, cut in half diagonally, for one C triangle
Red print #3	One 1½" x 1½" D square
Green print #1	One 4½" x 2½" B rectangle
Green print #2	One 2⅞" x 2⅞" square, cut in half diagonally, for one C triangle

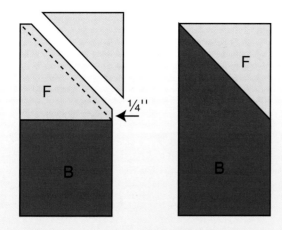

Figure 77. Sew a marked F square on one side of a red B rectangle.

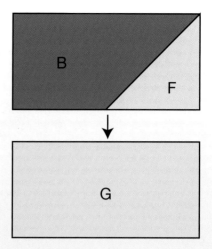

Figure 78. Unit 1 assembly, make one.

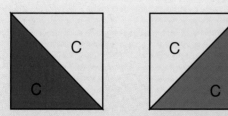

Figure 79. Make a blue/red and a blue/green C/C square.

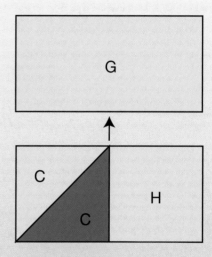

Figure 80. Unit 2 assembly, make one.

❦ Assembly ❦

1. Sign the A square as desired, referring to Signature Methods on pages 12–15. Take care to stay inside the ¼" seam allowances.

2. With a pencil, mark a diagonal line on the wrong side of two blue F squares. Right sides together, place one marked F square on one side of a red B

rectangle. Sew on the marked line. Trim the seam allowance to ¼" (Fig. 77, page 100). Open and press the seam allowance to the blue triangle. Trim the seam allowance of the dark fabric to ⅛" if necessary. Repeat this step with the green B rectangle.

3. Sew a blue G rectangle to the green and blue unit from step 2, completing Unit 1 (Fig. 78). Press the seam allowance toward the G rectangle.

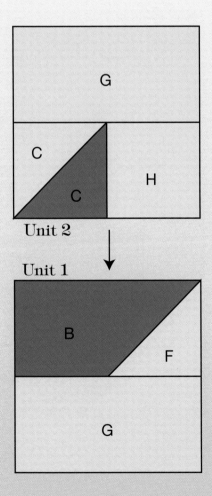

Unit 2

Unit 1

Figure 81. Sew units 1 and 2 together.

4. Sew a blue C triangle to the red C triangle. Sew a blue C triangle to the green C triangle (Fig. 79). Press the seam allowances toward the dark triangles.

5. Sew a blue H square to the green and blue C/C square from step 4. Sew this unit to a blue G rectangle, completing Unit 2 (Fig. 80). Press the seam allowance in the direction of the arrow.

6. Sew units 1 and 2 together as shown (Fig. 81). Press the seam allowance toward Unit 1.

7. Sew a blue D square to a red D square. Sew this unit to a blue E rectangle (Fig. 82, page 102). Press the seam allowance in the direction of the arrow.

8. Sew the unit from step 7 to the red and blue C/C square. Sew this unit to the red and blue F/B unit from step 2, completing Unit 3 (Fig. 83). Press the seam allowances in the direction of the arrows.

9. Sew Unit 3 to the A signature square. Press the seam allowance in the direction of the arrow. Sew the two halves of the block together, completing the block (Fig. 84, page 103).

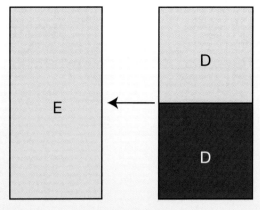

Figure 82. Sew a blue and red D
square together, then sew this to
a blue E rectangle.

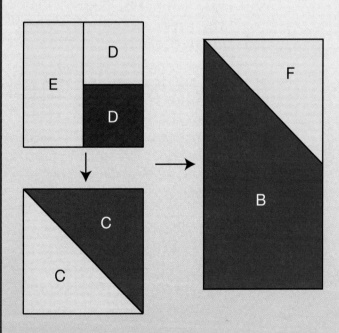

Figure 83. Unit 3 assembly

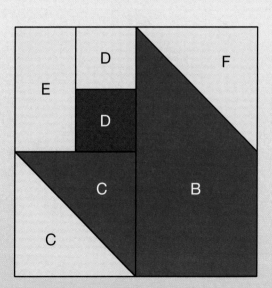

Unit 3

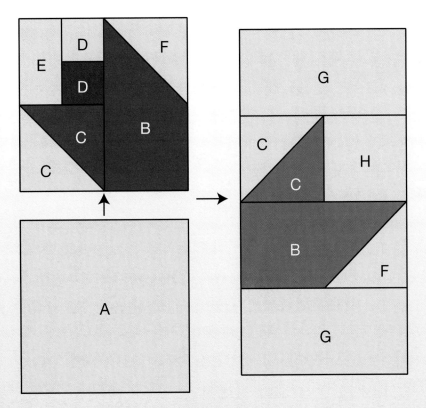

Figure 84. Block assembly

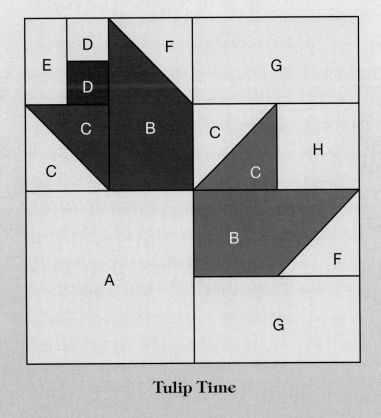

Tulip Time

Tulip Time

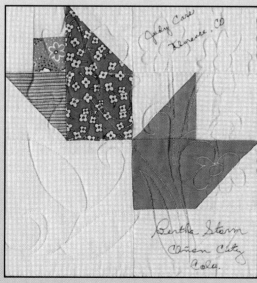

TULIP TIME, 42" x 48", made by the author and machine quilted by Judy Case, 2001. Members of the Royal Gorge Quilt Council signed the blocks.

Detail of the signature area in TULIP TIME

Finished Block Size: 4" x 4"

A Zigzag block set in a traditional strippy set can be very striking, with many patches for signatures and sentiments.

⫘ *Cutting* ⫘

Fabric	Pieces
Pale green solid	Two 2½" x 4½" signature A rectangles
Assorted pink prints	Four 2½" x 2½" B squares

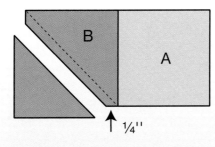

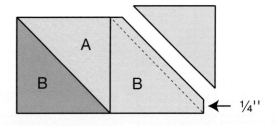

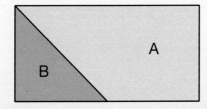

Figure 85. Sew a marked B square on one side of an A rectangle.

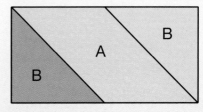

Figure 86. Unit 1 assembly, make one.

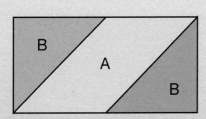

Figure 87. Unit 2 assembly, make one.

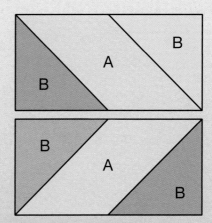

Figure 88. Block assembly

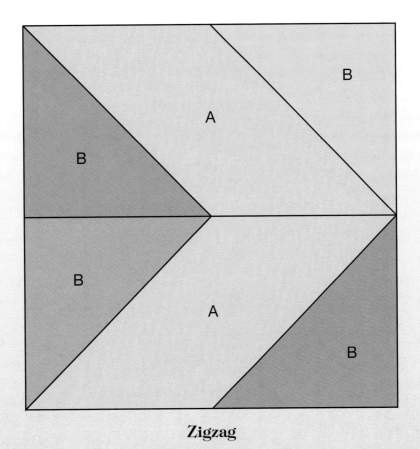

Zigzag

❧ *Assembly* ❧

1. With a pencil, draw a diagonal line on the wrong side of each pink B square. Place a B square on an A rectangle, right sides together, as shown. Sew on the diagonal line. Trim the seam allowance to ¼" (Fig. 85, page 106). Open and press the seam allowance toward the pink triangle.

2. Repeat step 1 with another pink square on the other side of the A rectangle, making sure that the stitching lines are parallel. Press the seam allowances

toward the B pieces to complete Unit 1 (Fig. 86).

3. Repeat steps 1 and 2 with the remaining A rectangle and B squares, but reverse the direction of the seams, completing Unit 2 (Fig. 87).

4. Sew units 1 and 2 together as shown, matching seams, to complete the block (Fig. 88). Press.

5. Sign the A parallelograms as desired, referring to Signature Methods on pages 12–15.

Zigzag

ZIGZAG, *53″ x 53″, made by the author. Some of the parallelograms in this quilt feature sentiments of friendship printed on the fabric by computer. The blocks are set in the traditional strippy style.*

Detail of signature area in ZIGZAG

Resources

C. Jenkins Necktie Co.
St. Louis, Missouri 63135
(314) 521-7544
www.home.il.net/
neckties/index.html

    Bubble Jet Set
    Bubble Jet Rinse

Polly's Pals
P.O. Box 890580
Temecula, California 92589
(906) 506-0466
www.pollyspals.com

    Stencils

Sakura Color Products of America
Hayward, California
www.gellyroll.com

    Pigma Micron Pens
    Identi-Pens

Sprinkles Sewing Center
Kathy and Jerry Binfet
802 South Main Street
Pueblo, Colorado 81004
(719) 544-2292
www.sprinklessewing.com

    Pfaff, Brother, and Viking
       sewing machines with
       digitizing software capability
    Viking printer fabric sheets for
       ink-jet printers and copiers

Tsukineko, Inc.
17640 NE 65th Street
Redmond, Washington 98052
(425) 883-7733
www.tsukineko.com

    Fabrico Pens
    Fabrico Multipurpose Craft Ink

Uchida of America, Corp.
3535 Del Amo Blvd.
Torrance, California 90503
(800) 541-5877
www.uchida.com

    Marvy fabric markers

Bibliography

Better Homes and Gardens. *Friendship
Quilting.* Des Moines, Iowa: Meredith
Corporation, 1990.

Kolter, Jane Bentley. *Forget Me Not, A
Gallery of Friendship and Album Quilts.*
Pittstown, New Jersey: The Main Street
Press, Inc., 1985.

Lipsett, Linda Otto. *Remember Me,
Women and Their Friendship Quilts.*
Lincolnwood, Illinois: The Quilt Digest
Press, 1985.

Orlovsky, Patsy and Myron. *Quilts in
America.* New York: McGraw-Hill Book
Company, 1974.

About the Author

Born into pioneering Colorado families, Sally Saulmon learned to quilt at an early age from her grandmothers. Her quilts have been exhibited throughout the United States and have appeared in numerous national publications. Sally lives in Cañon City, Colorado, with her husband, Bob. Their son, Michael, is a teacher, and their daughter, Jennifer, lives close by with her husband, Gary, and children, Caitlin and Wyatt.

Other AQS Books

This is only a small selection of the books available from the American Quilter's Society. AQS books are known worldwide for timely topics, clear writing, beautiful color photos, and accurate illustrations and patterns. The following books are available from your local bookseller, quilt shop, or public library.

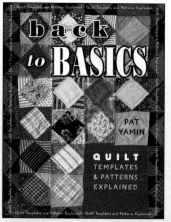

#6293   us$24.95

#6298   us$24.95

#6074   us$21.95

#6009   us$19.95

#5759   us$19.95

#5710   us$19.95

#4827   us$24.95

#6036   us$24.95

#3468   us$34.95

LOOK for these books nationally, CALL or VISIT our website at www.AQSquilt.com

1-800-626-5420